COMIC MNEMONICS FOR SPANISH VERBS

Cartoons and Mnemonic Phrases for the Spanish Language

Alacan Publishing
San Diego, California

Alacan Publishing
325 Canyonside Way Ste 262
Oceanside, CA 92058

sales@alacanpublishing.com
www.glasshousepress.com
www.alacanpublishing.com

Published in the United States by Glass House Press

ALACAN PUBLISHING is an imprint of Glass House Press. The Alacan Publishing name and logo are trademarks of Glass House Press.

COMIC MNEMONICS title is a trademark of Glass House Press.

The following trademarks appear in this book:
Levi's, Coneheads

Book Design by Arrow Graphics
Cover Design by George Foster

Sarris, Jim
Comic Mnemonics/Jim Harris

Illustrations: Patricia Nacher

ISBN-13: 978-0-9749096-3-9
LCCN: 20040902624

Printed in Canada on acid-free paper
14 13 12 11 10 09   3 4 5 6 7 8 9 10

ACKNOWLEDGMENT

Many people have played a role in the creation of the book. Their ideas and suggestions were the catalyst needed to find different ways to appeal to students. In particular, I'd like to thank Harriet Barnett for her workshops and constant reminders to never stop searching. Also, Dr. Mel Levine, author of *All Kinds of Minds*, who continues to encourage teachers and students to recognize and value different learning styles. Finally, Howard Gardner's theory of multiple intelligences gave me the first real way to determine student's strengths and weaknesses and to begin to address them in the classroom.

Also, thanks to my colleagues at Horace Greeley and Hackley who have helped with ideas, criticisms, encouragement and most of all, proofreading: Vita Materasso, Anna Reis, Maryse Santini, Mary Slavinski, Steve Warren, Christina DaCosta, Gerry Furey, John Hirsch, Steve Walker, Sue Moore, Carol Diguglielmo and Donna McBride.

To the members of the Self-Publishing discussion list at Yahoogroups, who patiently answered my many questions about publishing and marketing. I hope to be one of the people "answering" questions soon.

And last, but not least, there is my wife, Nina, and sons, Nicky and Cristian. Thanks for your patience and your honesty. Also, to José and María for allowing their mother, Patricia, the time to do all the illustrations.

TABLE OF CONTENTS

INTRODUCTION

Comic Mnemonics?

Here are some well-known facts: 60% of us are visual learners; we benefit from graphs, charts and diagrams in order to process and retain information. 30% of us are auditory learners; we need to hear it so that it stays in our mind and is easy to recall. By combining both approaches, a student dramatically increases his/her ability to memorize and later retrieve the information studied. Comic Mnemonics takes advantage of both styles to give the Spanish student what they need to succeed.

Named by the Greeks for memory-training 2500 years ago, mnemonics are methods, devices, or even mental tricks for improving memory. Many mnemonics are part of everyday culture, such as "I before E except after C", "Spring ahead, Fall back." A growing body of recent research indicates that these devices greatly aid memory retention.

The principle behind mnemonics is creating a cue that the student associates with what needs to be learned. For example, How many days does November have? Well, "thirty days hath September, April, June and November..."

Mnemonics don't necessarily need to rhyme: "Please excuse My Dear Aunt Sally (The order of operations in math: parenthesis, exponents, multiplication, division, addition, subtraction). They also don't need to be especially intellectual, "Eat **An As**pirin **Af**ter **A Na**ff **Sa**ndwich (The continents: Europe, Antartica, Asia, Africa, Australia, North America, South America). They just need to make a connection that allows the student to retain and later access the information more easily. The visual image adds to the mnemonic and gives the student extra help in retrieving the information.

Some visuals and phrases may be more helpful than others. Over the years, I have asked my own students their opinions. I have found that some students thought certain mnemonics were silly, while other students found them useful. The funniest part about the process was that the students who thought a particular visual was ridiculous ended up remembering it—just because it was ridiculous!

How does the process work?

A student sits down to write an essay and can't remember the word for "to sleep". Having practiced with Comic Mnemonics, she cues not only the visual of someone sleeping but also the phrase "Norm sleeps in the **dorm**." Ah ha!…Dormir!

The process works for reading as well as writing. The same student is reading and comes across the word "Alcanzar". The verb cues the phrase. "Al can reach his buddy Hal," which cues the visual—and the **ah ha** moment arrives…to reach!

Who should try this book?

Comic Mnemonics is for students who want or need another way to retain English and Spanish translations, beyond flash cards.

This book is intended to supplement—not replace—traditional vocabulary development, offering alternative ways to move between Spanish and English.

How to get the most out of this book:

Since we seldom need to memorize 100 verbs at a time, begin by referring to the verbs that you need at the moment, or the ones that constantly give you trouble. There's a list of verbs at the end of the book. Review the list quickly to see what verbs you need to practice and which ones you already know.

HOW TO USE
THIS BOOK

How each page is set up

Each verb has the same set-up both on the main page and on the one that follows.

On the main page: Students have the visual and the mnemonic phrase to look at and assimilate. The verb and definition are centered at the top in large, bold print. A small drawing at the top right gives the phonetic pronunciation of the verb. This little drawing can also be used to leaf through the book and quickly quiz yourself without looking at the whole page. At the bottom of the main page are the conjugations in the present and past tense. (You'll find a more extensive grammar review at the end of the book). In the middle, the main graphic creates a visual cue. Above the graphic are the key phase, definition, and the Spanish verb; a mnemonic phrase runs as a caption below the illustration.

On the following page: The main visual is repeated along with some practice exercises. And you can practice recalling the translation of the verb in English.

LIST OF VERBS

Abrir	Alcanzar	Almorzar	Alquilar	Aprender
Arreglar	Asistir	Atender	Ayudar	Bailar
Beber	Buscar	Caerse	Cambiar	Caminar
Cantar	Cenar	Cerrar	Cocinar	Comenzar
Comer	Comprar	Comprender	Conducir	Conocer
Construir	Contestar	Correr	Cortar	Creer
Cruzar	Cubrir	Dar	Decir	Dejar
Descansar	Despertarse	Dormir	Durar	Encontrar
Enfermarse	Escribir	Escuchar	Esperar	Estudiar
Evitar	Fumar	Ganar	Gastar	Gritar
Hablar	Hacer	Ir	Jugar	Levantarse
Lavarse	Leer	Limpiar	Llamar	Llegar
Llevar	Mandar	Meter	Mirar	Nadar
Odiar	Oír	Pagar	Parar	Pedir
Pegar	Pensar	Perder	Poner	Preguntar
Prometer	Querer	Recibir	Recordar	Robar
Saber	Sacar	Salir	Saludar	Subir
Suspender	Tener	Terminar	Tirar	Tocar
Tomar	Trabajar	Traer	Vender	Venir
Ver	Viajar	Vivir	Volar	Volver

ABRIR
to open

ah-brear

KEYWORD:
Abracadabra…***open***
Abrir

Abracadabra, **abr**acaday…***open*** the door right away!

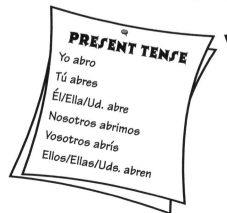

PRESENT TENSE

Yo abro

Tú abres

Él/Ella/Ud. abre

Nosotros abrimos

Vosotros abrís

Ellos/Ellas/Uds. abren

PRETERITE TENSE

Yo abrí

Tú abriste

Él/Ella/Ud. abrió

Nosotros abrimos

Vosotros abristeis

Ellos/Ellas/Uds. abrieron

ABRIR

THE PRESENT TENSE	THE PRETERITE TENSE
Yo _____ la puerta.	Él _____ el regalo ayer.
Ella _____ la ventana.	Ellos no _____ la carta anoche.
Nosotros no _____ el libro.	Tú _____ la maleta.
¿ _____ Uds. el armario?	¿ _____ Elena el sobre?
Tú _____ la caja.	Yo _____ el cuarto.

ALCANZAR
to reach

ahl-kahn-zahr

KEYWORD:
Al can...*reach*
Alcanzar

Al **can** <u>reach</u> his buddy Hal

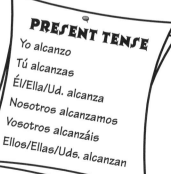

PRESENT TENSE
Yo alcanzo
Tú alcanzas
Él/Ella/Ud. alcanza
Nosotros alcanzamos
Vosotros alcanzáis
Ellos/Ellas/Uds. alcanzan

PRETERITE TENSE
Yo alcancé
Tú alcanzaste
Él/Ella/Ud. alcanzó
Nosotros alcanzamos
Vosotros alcanzasteis
Ellos/Ellas/Uds. alcanzaron

ALCANZAR

THE PRESENT TENSE	THE PRETERITE TENSE
Ella _____ la pelota.	Mario _____ la botella.
Nosotros _____ las llaves.	Los niños no _____ los dulces.
Ud. no _____ los zapatos.	Tú _____ los premios.
¿ _____ tú el autobús?	¿ _____ ellas las entradas?
Yo _____ los papeles.	Yo no _____ la caja.

ALMORZAR

ahl-mohr-zahr

to eat lunch

KEYWORD:
Al More...*eats lunch*
Almorzar

Al More *eats lunch* with Al Less

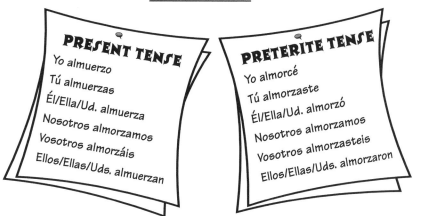

PRESENT TENSE

Yo almuerzo
Tú almuerzas
Él/Ella/Ud. almuerza
Nosotros almorzamos
Vosotros almorzáis
Ellos/Ellas/Uds. almuerzan

PRETERITE TENSE

Yo almorcé
Tú almorzaste
Él/Ella/Ud. almorzó
Nosotros almorzamos
Vosotros almorzasteis
Ellos/Ellas/Uds. almorzaron

ALMORZAR

THE PRESENT TENSE	THE PRETERITE TENSE
Yo _____ a las dos.	Juan no _____ ayer.
Nosotros no _____ en la cafetería.	La semana pasada tú _____ en casa.
Ella _____ con Miguel.	Yo _____ con mi familia.
¿ _____ Uds. en la tienda?	Ellos _____ tarde.
Tú _____ conmigo.	Pedro no _____ con sus amigos.

ALQUILAR
to rent

KEYWORD:
Al Key...*rents*
Alquilar

Al Key ___rents___ cars from Mars

PRESENT TENSE
Yo alquilo
Tú alquilas
Él/Ella/Ud. alquila
Nosotros alquilamos
Vosotros alquiláis
Ellos/Ellas/Uds. alquilan

PRETERITE TENSE
Yo alquilé
Tú alquilaste
Él/Ella/Ud. alquiló
Nosotros alquilamos
Vosotros alquilasteis
Ellos/Ellas/Uds. alquilaron

ALQUILAR

THE PRESENT TENSE	THE PRETERITE TENSE
Ella _____ el coche.	Ayer él _____ la casa.
Ellos no _____ la moto.	Nosotros _____ las luces.
¿ _____ tú la película?	¿ _____ Ud. la computadora?
Nosotros _____ la máquina.	Yo _____ el teléfono móvil.
Yo _____ el autobús.	Ellas _____ el barco.

APRENDER
to learn

ah-prehn-dehr

KEYWORD:
Apprentice...***learns***
Aprender

The **appren**tice **learns** to be a dentist

PRESENT TENSE
Yo aprendo
Tú aprendes
Él/Ella/Ud. aprende
Nosotros aprendemos
Vosotros aprendéis
Ellos/Ellas/Uds. aprenden

PRETERITE TENSE
Yo aprendí
Tú aprendiste
Él/Ella/Ud. aprendió
Nosotros aprendimos
Vosotros aprendisteis
Ellos/Ellas/Uds. aprendieron

APRENDER

THE PRESENT TENSE	THE PRETERITE TENSE
Yo _____ mucho en la clase.	Los estudiantes _____ del libro nuevo.
Ellas no _____ nada con la profesora nueva.	Yo _____ poco.
Nosotros _____ de la televisión.	¿ _____ él de su padre?
¿ _____ tú en la escuela?	Miguel _____ los verbos.
Pablo no _____ si no estudia.	Tú _____ español con tus padres.

ARREGLAR
to fix

ah-rreh-glahr

KEYWORD:
A regular…**fix**
Arreglar

Meyer can't **fix** it with **a reg**ular tire

PRESENT TENSE
Yo arreglo
Tú arreglas
Él/Ella/Ud. arregla
Nosotros arreglamos
Vosotros arregláis
Ellos/Ellas/Uds. arreglan

PRETERITE TENSE
Yo arreglé
Tú arreglaste
Él/Ella/Ud. arregló
Nosotros arreglamos
Vosotros arreglasteis
Ellos/Ellas/Uds. arreglaron

ARREGLAR

THE PRESENT TENSE	THE PRETERITE TENSE
Él _____ el coche.	Anoche nosotros _____ la bañera.
Nosotros _____ el cuarto.	Mi padre _____ el horno.
Uds. no _____ las tuberías.	¿ _____ tú la ventana?
¿ _____ ella el asunto?	Los mecánicos no _____ el motor.
Tú _____ la moto.	Yo _____ la computadora.

ASISTIR
to attend

ah-sees-teer

KEYWORD:
Assistant...**_attends_**
Asistir

The **assist**ant, Joe Best, **_attends_** the games formally dressed

PRESENT TENSE
Yo asisto

Tú asistes

Él/Ella/Ud. asiste

Nosotros asistimos

Vosotros asistís

Ellos/Ellas/Uds. asisten

PRETERITE TENSE
Yo asistí

Tú asististe

Él/Ella/Ud. asistió

Nosotros asistimos

Vosotros asististeis

Ellos/Ellas/Uds. asistieron

ASISTIR

THE PRESENT TENSE	THE PRETERITE TENSE
Ella _____ al concierto.	Uds. _____ a la ópera.
Yo _____ a la clase.	Tú no _____ a la reunión.
¿ _____ ellos a la fiesta?	Los profesores _____ al debate.
Tú _____ al baile.	¿ _____ ella a la ceremonia?
Nosotros no _____ a la conferencia.	Yo no _____ al bautizo.

ATENDER
to attend to

ah-tehn-dehr

KEYWORD:
attendant...***attends to***
atender

The **attend**ant ***attends to*** people's nourishment

PRESENT TENSE
Yo atiendo
Tú atiendes
Él/Ella/Ud. atiende
Nosotros atendemos
Vosotros atendéis
Ellos/Ellas/Uds. atienden

PRETERITE TENSE
Yo atendí
Tú atendiste
Él/Ella/Ud. atendió
Nosotros atendimos
Vosotros atendisteis
Ellos/Ellas/Uds. atendieron

ATENDER

THE PRESENT TENSE	THE PRETERITE TENSE
Él _____ a los pacientes.	Ellos no _____ a los padres.
Ellas _____ a los niños.	Yo _____ a los estudiantes.
Tú _____ a los jefes.	¿ _____ tú a los pilotos?
¿ _____ Uds. a los profesores?	El jefe no _____ a los clientes.
Yo no _____ a los enfermos.	Nosotros _____ a los invitados.

AYUDAR
to help

ah-yoo-**dahr**

KEYWORD:
Ay..you...*help*
Ayudar

Ay..you...little ***help*** with my hairdoo!

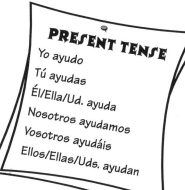

PRESENT TENSE

Yo ayudo
Tú ayudas
Él/Ella/Ud. ayuda
Nosotros ayudamos
Vosotros ayudáis
Ellos/Ellas/Uds. ayudan

PRETERITE TENSE

Yo ayudé
Tú ayudaste
Él/Ella/Ud. ayudó
Nosotros ayudamos
Vosotros ayudasteis
Ellos/Ellas/Uds. ayudaron

AYUDAR

THE PRESENT TENSE	THE PRETERITE TENSE
Tú _____ en la clase.	Él no _____ ayer.
Ella no _____ a su padre.	Nosotros _____ durante la fiesta.
¿ _____ ellos a los amigos?	¿ _____ Uds. anoche?
Nosotros _____ con el trabajo.	Yo _____ a mi hermano.
Yo no _____ con la tarea.	Tú _____ a tu madre.

BAILAR
to dance

bah-ee-larhr

KEYWORD:
Bailarina...*dances*
Bailar

Marina, the **bailar**ina, *dances*

PRESENT TENSE
Yo bailo

Tú bailas

Él/Ella/Ud. baila

Nosotros bailamos

Vosotros bailáis

Ellos/Ellas/Uds. bailan

PRETERITE TENSE
Yo bailé

Tú bailaste

Él/Ella/Ud. bailó

Nosotros bailamos

Vosotros bailasteis

Ellos/Ellas/Uds. bailaron

BAILAR

THE PRESENT TENSE	THE PRETERITE TENSE
Ella _____ sola.	Ellos _____ juntos.
Nosotros _____ la bamba.	Yo _____ la salsa.
Yo _____ con mi novia.	¿ _____ Juan con su madre?
¿ _____ tú durante la fiesta?	Nosotros no _____ en el club.
Ud. _____ todos los días.	Las chicas _____ en la casa.

BEBER
to drink

beh-behr

KEYWORD:
Bebé...*drinks*
Beber

The **bebé *drinks*** a latté

PRESENT TENSE

Yo bebo

Tú bebes

Él/Ella/Ud. bebe

Nosotros bebemos

Vosotros bebéis

Ellos/Ellas/Uds. beben

PRETERITE TENSE

Yo bebí

Tú bebiste

Él/Ella/Ud. bebió

Nosotros bebimos

Vosotros bebisteis

Ellos/Ellas/Uds. bebieron

BEBER

THE PRESENT TENSE	THE PRETERITE TENSE
Yo no _____ coca-cola.	Él no _____ la sangría.
Ellas _____ los refrescos.	Nosotros _____ mucho jugo de manzana.
¿ _____ tú la leche?	Ellas no _____ con los niños.
Nosotros _____ agua todos los días.	¿ _____ tú el vaso de agua?
Manolo no _____ por la mañana.	Yo no _____ el champán.

BUSCAR
to look for

boos-kahr

KEYWORD:
bus..._looks for_
buscar

Gus _looks for_ the **bus**

boos-kahr

PRESENT TENSE
Yo busco
Tú buscas
Él/Ella/Ud. busca
Nosotros buscamos
Vosotros buscáis
Ellos/Ellas/Uds. buscan

PRETERITE TENSE
Yo busqué
Tú buscaste
Él/Ella/Ud. buscó
Nosotros buscamos
Vosotros buscasteis
Ellos/Ellas/Uds. buscaron

BUSCAR

THE PRESENT TENSE	THE PRETERITE TENSE
Tú _____ las llaves.	Yo no _____ la información.
Yo _____ mi libro.	Ella _____ a Pepe.
¿ _____ ellos el mapa?	¿ _____ tú los libros?
Nosotros _____ la casa.	Mi amigo no _____ su raqueta.
Mario _____ su coche.	Sus primos _____ las fotos.

CAERSE
to fall down

kah-**ehr**-seh

KEYWORD:
Cae**sar**...**_falls down_**
Caerse

Everyday, **Cae**sar **_falls down_** the same stairway

PRESENT TENSE
Yo me caigo
Tú te caes
Él/Ella/Ud. se cae
Nosotros nos caemos
Vosotros os caéis
Ellos/Ellas/Uds. se caen

PRETERITE TENSE
Yo me caí
Tú te caíste
Él/Ella/Ud. se cayó
Nosotros nos caímos
Vosotros os caísteis
Ellos/Ellas/Uds. se cayeron

CAERSE

THE PRESENT TENSE	THE PRETERITE TENSE
Yo _____ en el jardín.	Anoche yo _____ en la calle.
Ella _____ en la casa.	Nosotros _____ en la nieve.
Nosotros _____ cada mañana.	Uds. _____ esta mañana.
Ellos no _____ por la escalera.	¿ _____ José por la lluvia?
¿ _____ tú mucho?	Tú _____ la semana pasada.

CAMBIAR
to change

kahm-bee-yahr

KEYWORD:
combo...**_changed_**
cambiar

No way! The school **_changed_** the **comb**o again today!

PRESENT TENSE

Yo cambio

Tú cambias

Él/Ella/Ud. cambia

Nosotros cambiamos

Vosotros cambiáis

Ellos/Ellas/Uds. cambian

PRETERITE TENSE

Yo cambié

Tú cambiaste

Él/Ella/Ud. cambió

Nosotros cambiamos

Vosotros cambiasteis

Ellos/Ellas/Uds. cambiaron

CAMBIAR

THE PRESENT TENSE	THE PRETERITE TENSE
Ellas no _____ el dinero.	Yo no _____ la fecha.
Nosotros _____ los pantalones.	Mis amigos _____ los regalos.
Yo _____ el reloj.	¿ _____ tú las camisas?
¿ _____ él las televisiones?	Él _____ los papeles.
Tú _____ el número de teléfono.	Uds. no _____ los libros.

CAMINAR
to walk

kah-mee-nahr

KEYWORD:
cam el... **walks**
caminar

KEYWORD:
cam el... **walks**
caminar

Mark **walks** his **cam**el in the park

PRESENT TENSE

Yo camino

Tú caminas

Él/Ella/Ud. camina

Nosotros caminamos

Vosotros camináis

Ellos/Ellas/Uds. caminan

PRETERITE TENSE

Yo caminé

Tú caminaste

Él/Ella/Ud. caminó

Nosotros caminamos

Vosotros caminasteis

Ellos/Ellas/Uds. caminaron

CAMINAR

THE PRESENT TENSE	THE PRETERITE TENSE
Nosotros _____ al parque.	Yo _____ por la playa.
Ellos _____ a la tienda.	Ella no _____ rápido.
¿ _____ ella a la escuela?	¿ _____ Uds. al cine?
Tú _____ con tus amigos.	Tú _____ con tu perro.
Uds. no _____ al centro.	Nosotros _____ con la policía.

CANTAR
to sing

kahn-tahr

KEYWORD:
can't...*sing*
cantar

Bing **can't *sing!***

PRESENT TENSE

Yo canto

Tú cantas

Él/Ella/Ud. canta

Nosotros cantamos

Vosotros cantáis

Ellos/Ellas/Uds. cantan

PRETERITE TENSE

Yo canté

Tú cantaste

Él/Ella/Ud. cantó

Nosotros cantamos

Vosotros cantasteis

Ellos/Ellas/Uds. cantaron

CANTAR

THE PRESENT TENSE	THE PRETERITE TENSE
Ella _____ en el coro.	Ellos _____ anoche en la fiesta.
Uds. _____ en español.	Ud. _____ con sus amigos ayer.
Yo no _____ por la mañana.	¿ _____ Miguel en la clase?
¿ _____ tú en la ducha?	Nosotros _____ la nueva canción.
Nosotros _____ muy bien.	Yo _____ muy mal durante el concierto.

CENAR
to eat dinner

seh-nahr

KEYWORD:
centipede…**_eating dinner_**
cenar

Centipedes **_eating dinner_**

PRESENT TENSE

Yo ceno

Tú cenas

Él/Ella/Ud. cena

Nosotros cenamos

Vosotros cenáis

Ellos/Ellas/Uds. cenan

PRETERITE TENSE

Yo cené

Tú cenaste

Él/Ella/Ud. cenó

Nosotros cenamos

Vosotros cenasteis

Ellos/Ellas/Uds. cenaron

CENAR

THE PRESENT TENSE	THE PRETERITE TENSE
Yo _____ con mi familia.	Tú _____ mucho ayer.
Ellas _____ muy tarde.	Ud. _____ con sus padres anoche.
Uds. no _____ en el restaurante.	¿ _____ ellos en el comedor?
¿ _____ él con su novia?	Yo _____ muy temprano
Nosotros _____ pasta todas las noches.	Mis primos no _____ juntos.

CERRAR
to close

seh-rrahr

KEYWORD:
certainly..._**closed**_
cerrar

He **cer**tainly _**closed**_ that door for sure!

PRESENT TENSE
Yo cierro

Tú cierras

Él/Ella/Ud. cierra

Nosotros cerramos

Vosotros cerráis

Ellos/Ellas/Uds. cierran

PRETERITE TENSE
Yo cerré

Tú cerraste

Él/Ella/Ud. cerró

Nosotros cerramos

Vosotros cerrasteis

Ellos/Ellas/Uds. cerraron

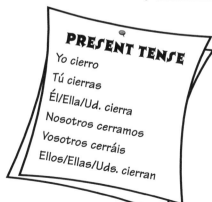

CERRAR

THE PRESENT TENSE	THE PRETERITE TENSE
Ella no _____ la puerta.	Yo no _____ la maleta.
Tú _____ el libro después de leer.	¿ _____ ellos la nevera?
Yo _____ la ventana cuando tengo frío.	Nosotros _____ la cartera.
¿ _____ él la caja?	Él _____ el microondas.
Nosotros _____ la casa.	Tú _____ el cajón.

COCINAR
to cook

koh-see-nahr

KEYWORD:
coco-cola...**_cooks_**
cocinar

Lola **_cooks_** using **COC**o-cola

PRESENT TENSE
Yo cocino

Tú cocinas

Él/Ella/Ud. cocina

Nosotros cocinamos

Vosotros cocináis

Ellos/Ellas/Uds. cocinan

PRETERITE TENSE
Yo cociné

Tú cocinaste

Él/Ella/Ud. cocinó

Nosotros cocinamos

Vosotros cocinasteis

Ellos/Ellas/Uds. cocinaron

COCINAR

THE PRESENT TENSE	THE PRETERITE TENSE
Ella _____ la carne.	Mario _____ anoche.
Nosotros _____ las patatas.	Los niños no _____ los huevos.
Ud. no _____ mucho.	Ud. _____ para ella.
¿_____ tú todos los días?	¿_____ tú hamburguesas?
Yo _____ con mi madre.	Yo no _____ esta mañana.

COMENZAR
to begin

koh-mehn-sahr

ONCE UPON A TIME...

KEYWORD:
comen*ce*...**begin**
comenzar

BEGIN
COMENCE THE TEST

Aah! **Comen***ce*...**begin,** it's all the same you ding-a-ling!

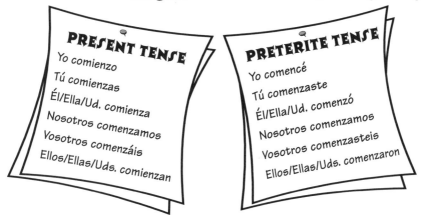

PRESENT TENSE

Yo comienzo

Tú comienzas

Él/Ella/Ud. comienza

Nosotros comenzamos

Vosotros comenzáis

Ellos/Ellas/Uds. comienzan

PRETERITE TENSE

Yo comencé

Tú comenzaste

Él/Ella/Ud. comenzó

Nosotros comenzamos

Vosotros comenzasteis

Ellos/Ellas/Uds. comenzaron

COMENZAR

THE PRESENT TENSE	THE PRETERITE TENSE
Ella _____la clase ahora.	Él _____ el examen hace cinco minutos.
Nosotros _____ la lección a las dos.	Ellos _____ a escribir el poema.
Tú _____ el libro mañana.	¿ _____ tú el proyecto?
¿ _____ ellos el concierto?	Nosotros _____ a trabajar en el jardín.
Yo _____ mi curso la semana que viene.	Yo _____ el ensayo con mi profesor.

COMER
to eat

koh-mehr

KEYWORD:
com...*eating*
comer

www.**eating**.com

PRESENT TENSE

Yo como

Tú comes

Él/Ella/Ud. come

Nosotros comemos

Vosotros coméis

Ellos/Ellas/Uds. comen

PRETERITE TENSE

Yo comí

Tú comiste

Él/Ella/Ud. comió

Nosotros comimos

Vosotros comisteis

Ellos/Ellas/Uds. comieron

COMER

THE PRESENT TENSE	THE PRETERITE TENSE
Yo _____ a las tres.	Nosotros _____ los tacos.
Ellos no _____ frutas.	¿ _____ ellos a las seis?
¿ _____ Ud. los postres?	Miguel no _____ la carne.
Nosotros _____ los pasteles.	Los niños _____ los vegetales.
Ella _____ con su padre.	Yo _____ toda la comida de la fiesta.

COMPRAR
to buy

kohm-prahr

KEYWORD:
computer...*buys*
comprar

My tutor *__buys__* a **comp**uter

PRESENT TENSE

Yo compro
Tú compras
Él/Ella/Ud. compra
Nosotros compramos
Vosotros compráis
Ellos/Ellas/Uds. compran

PRETERITE TENSE

Yo compré
Tú compraste
Él/Ella/Ud. compró
Nosotros compramos
Vosotros comprasteis
Ellos/Ellas/Uds. compraron

COMPRAR

THE PRESENT TENSE	THE PRETERITE TENSE
Yo _____ la ropa en la tienda.	Tú _____ la computadora para Ana.
Ellos no _____ comida en el supermercado.	Ellos no _____ el reloj.
¿Dónde _____ tú los zapatos?	¿ _____ Elena la casa?
Nosotros no _____ nada los domingos.	Yo _____ el billete a España.
Ella _____ su coche mañana.	Los estudiantes _____ sus libros ayer.

COMPRENDER

kohm-prehn-dehr

to understand

KEYWORD:
comprehend...**understand**
comprender

Understand...**compre**hend...it's all the same in the end!

PRESENT TENSE

Yo comprendo
Tú comprendes
Él/Ella/Ud. comprende
Nosotros comprendemos
Vosotros comprendéis
Ellos/Ellas/Uds. comprenden

PRETERITE TENSE

Yo comprendí
Tú comprendiste
Él/Ella/Ud. comprendió
Nosotros comprendimos
Vosotros comprendisteis
Ellos/Ellas/Uds. comprendieron

COMPRENDER

THE PRESENT TENSE	THE PRETERITE TENSE
Ella no _____ nada.	Yo no _____ lo que ella dijo.
Nosotros _____ todo lo que dice el profesor.	Ud. _____ el significado del mensaje.
Uds. _____ las matemáticas.	Nosotros _____ la lección.
¿ _____ tú la situación?	¿ _____ tú el nuevo concepto?
Yo _____ que hay un problema.	Los estudiantes _____ el anuncio.

CONDUCIR
to drive

kohn-doo-seer

KEYWORD:
conductor... _**drives**_
conducir

El **conduc**tor _**drives**_ the instructors

PRESENT TENSE

Yo conduzco
Tú conduces
Él/Ella/Ud. conduce
Nosotros conducimos
Vosotros conducís
Ellos/Ellas/Uds. conducen

PRETERITE TENSE

Yo conduje
Tú condujiste
Él/Ella/Ud. condujo
Nosotros condujimos
Vosotros condujisteis
Ellos/Ellas/Uds. condujeron

CONDUCIR

THE PRESENT TENSE	THE PRETERITE TENSE
Ella _____ por la noche.	Uds. _____ al concierto.
Yo no _____ porque me da miedo.	Yo _____ a la escuela.
Ellos _____ al parque.	Ella _____ la ambulancia.
¿ _____ Ud. el coche grande?	¿ _____ tú toda la noche?
Tú no _____ con tu padre.	Marta y Juan _____ a Florida.

CONOCER
to know

koh-noh-**sehr**

Ed **_knows_** the **con**eheads©

PRESENT TENSE

Yo conozco
Tú conoces
Él/Ella/Ud. conoce
Nosotros conocemos
Vosotros conocéis
Ellos/Ellas/Uds. conocen

PRETERITE TENSE

Yo conocí
Tú conociste
Él/Ella/Ud. conoció
Nosotros conocimos
Vosotros conocisteis
Ellos/Ellas/Uds. conocieron

CONOCER

THE PRESENT TENSE	THE PRETERITE TENSE
Yo _____ al presidente.	Nosotros _____ a un actor famoso ayer.
Ella no _____ a su profesor.	Ella no _____ al dueño del hotel.
Nosotros _____ Boston muy bien.	¿Dónde _____ tú a Juan?
¿ _____ ellos un restaurante bueno?	Yo _____ a Ana en una fiesta.
Tú _____ al jefe del departamento.	Ellos _____ al médico anoche.

CONSTRUIR
to build

kohn-stru-eer

KEYWORD:
constructed...**building**
construir

I **constru**cted this **building** with gold gilding

PRESENT TENSE

Yo construyo
Tú construyes
Él/Ella/Ud. construye
Nosotros construimos
Vosotros construís
Ellos/Ellas/Uds. construyen

PRETERITE TENSE

Yo construí
Tú construiste
Él/Ella/Ud. construyó
Nosotros construimos
Vosotros construisteis
Ellos/Ellas/Uds. construyeron

CONSTRUIR

THE PRESENT TENSE	THE PRETERITE TENSE
Ellos _____ casas de lujo.	Ella _____ la pared detrás de su casa.
Nosotros _____ un castillo en la arena.	¿ _____ ellos los hoteles en la playa?
Pedro _____ el gimnasio primero.	Yo _____ las sillas en mi sala.
¿Dónde _____ tú el proyecto?	Miguel no _____ las camas.
Yo _____ mucho en mi tiempo libre.	Nosotros _____ un restaurante en el centro.

CONTESTAR

kohn-tehs-tahr

to answer

KEYWORD:
contestant... ***answers***
contestar

The **contest**ant ***answers*** the questions

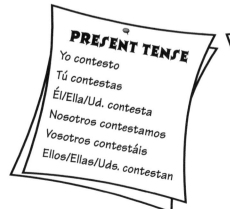

PRESENT TENSE

Yo contesto
Tú contestas
Él/Ella/Ud. contesta
Nosotros contestamos
Vosotros contestáis
Ellos/Ellas/Uds. contestan

PRETERITE TENSE

Yo contesté
Tú contestaste
Él/Ella/Ud. contestó
Nosotros contestamos
Vosotros contestasteis
Ellos/Ellas/Uds. contestaron

CONTESTAR

THE PRESENT TENSE	THE PRETERITE TENSE
Ella no _____ la pregunta.	Uds. _____ la carta.
Nosotros _____ en inglés.	¿Cuándo _____ tú al jefe?
¿ _____ ellos a tiempo?	Yo no _____ el teléfono.
Tú _____ una pregunta difícil.	Mi amigo _____ la llamada.
Yo _____ a menudo en la clase.	Nosotros _____ las peticiones.

CORRER
to run

koh-rrehr

KEYWORD:
corridor...**_run_**
correr

"Don't **_run_** in the **corr**idor, son!"

PRESENT TENSE

Yo corro

Tú corres

Él/Ella/Ud. corre

Nosotros corremos

Vosotros corréis

Ellos/Ellas/Uds. corren

PRETERITE TENSE

Yo corrí

Tú corriste

Él/Ella/Ud. corrió

Nosotros corrimos

Vosotros corristeis

Ellos/Ellas/Uds. corrieron

CORRER

THE PRESENT TENSE	THE PRETERITE TENSE
Ella no _____ en el parque.	Ellas _____ en la carrera.
Nosotros _____ cada mañana.	Él _____ con su equipo.
¿Cuándo _____ ellos?	Tú _____ un maratón.
Yo _____ con mis amigos.	¿A qué hora _____ Uds.?
Tú _____ muy rápido.	Yo _____ antes de ir a la escuela.

CORTAR
to cut

kohr-tahr

KEYWORD:
cord...cut
cortar

"Don't **cut** the **cor**d, my Lord!"

PRESENT TENSE

Yo corto

Tú cortas

Él/Ella/Ud. corta

Nosotros cortamos

Vosotros cortáis

Ellos/Ellas/Uds. cortan

PRETERITE TENSE

Yo corté

Tú cortaste

Él/Ella/Ud. cortó

Nosotros cortamos

Vosotros cortasteis

Ellos/Ellas/Uds. cortaron

CORTAR

THE PRESENT TENSE	THE PRETERITE TENSE
Yo _____ el papel.	Tú no _____ el dedo.
Él no _____ la pizza.	¿Qué _____ ellos?
¿Cuándo _____ tú el diseño?	Yo _____ los cables.
Nosotros_____ la cuerda por la tarde.	Mis abuelos _____ su pelo.
Uds. _____ la madera.	Nosotros _____ los lazos.

CREER
to believe

kreh-ehr

KEYWORD:
creepy...**_believe_**
creer

"**_Believe_** me, you're **cree**py!"

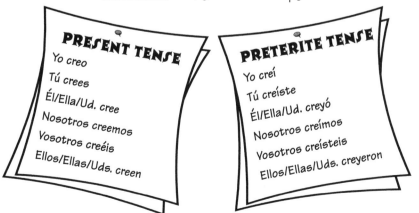

PRESENT TENSE
Yo creo

Tú crees

Él/Ella/Ud. cree

Nosotros creemos

Vosotros creéis

Ellos/Ellas/Uds. creen

PRETERITE TENSE
Yo creí

Tú creíste

Él/Ella/Ud. creyó

Nosotros creímos

Vosotros creísteis

Ellos/Ellas/Uds. creyeron

CREER

THE PRESENT TENSE	THE PRETERITE TENSE
Yo no _____ la historia.	Ud. _____ la explicación.
Ellos _____ a Miguel.	Tú _____ la carta.
Nosotros _____ al profesor.	¿ _____ ellos la novela?
¿ _____ tú la excusa?	Yo no _____ la información.
Ella no _____ a su marido.	Marta _____ lo que oyó.

CRUZAR
to cross

kroo-sahr

KEYWORD:
cru**ise**...***crosses***
cruzar

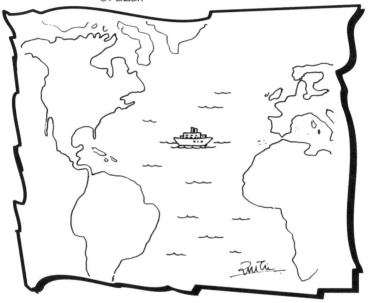

The **cru**ise ship ***crosses*** the ocean

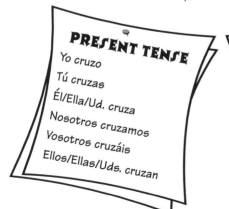

PRESENT TENSE
Yo cruzo
Tú cruzas
Él/Ella/Ud. cruza
Nosotros cruzamos
Vosotros cruzáis
Ellos/Ellas/Uds. cruzan

PRETERITE TENSE
Yo crucé
Tú cruzaste
Él/Ella/Ud. cruzó
Nosotros cruzamos
Vosotros cruzasteis
Ellos/Ellas/Uds. cruzaron

CRUZAR

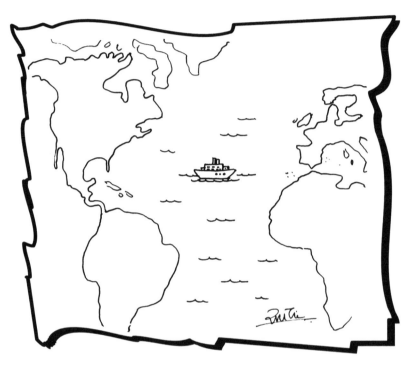

THE PRESENT TENSE	THE PRETERITE TENSE
Marcos _____ la calle.	Ella _____ la carretera.
Nosotros no _____ el puente.	Uds. _____ el patio.
¿ _____ ellos el sendero?	¿ _____ Mario el Atlántico?
Tú _____ la ciudad.	Nosotros _____ el aparcamiento.
Uds. _____ el campo.	Yo _____ la pista.

CUBRIR
to cover

koo-**breer**

Mother bear **_covers_** her **cub**s with care

PRESENT TENSE
Yo cubro

Tú cubres

Él/Ella/Ud. cubre

Nosotros cubrimos

Vosotros cubrís

Ellos/Ellas/Uds. cubren

PRETERITE TENSE
Yo cubrí

Tú cubriste

Él/Ella/Ud. cubrió

Nosotros cubrimos

Vosotros cubristeis

Ellos/Ellas/Uds. cubrieron

CUBRIR

THE PRESENT TENSE	THE PRETERITE TENSE
Nosotros _____ la cama.	Él _____ el barco ayer.
Ella _____ el coche.	¿ _____ tú el patio?
¿ _____ tú el sofá?	Ellos _____ la computadora.
Uds. _____ las bicicletas.	Nosotros _____ los papeles.
Yo no _____ la mesa.	Yo _____ la nevera.

DAR
to give

dahr

KEYWORD:
darts...**_give_**
dar

"Hey Bart, **_give_** me the **dar**ts!"

PRESENT TENSE
Yo doy
Tú das
Él/Ella/Ud. da
Nosotros damos
Vosotros dais
Ellos/Ellas/Uds. dan

PRETERITE TENSE
Yo di
Tú diste
Él/Ella/Ud. dio
Nosotros dimos
Vosotros disteis
Ellos/Ellas/Uds. dieron

DAR

THE PRESENT TENSE	THE PRETERITE TENSE
Ellos _____ su dinero a la iglesia.	Nosotros _____ el coche a José.
Nosotros _____ las camisas a los vecinos.	Ella _____ comida a los pobres.
¿ _____ ella su tarea a la profesora?	Yo no _____ la información a la policia.
Yo_____ mis zapatos a mi hermana.	¿ _____ Uds. las llaves a Miguel?
Tú _____ ayuda a tus compañeros.	Tú _____ el anillo a tu novia.

DECIR
to say (to tell)

deh-seer

KEYWORD:
decir..._said_
decir

If I've **_said_** it once, I've **_said_** it a thousand times. **Decir** is to **_say_** (and **_to tell_** at times)

PRESENT TENSE
Yo digo
Tú dices
Él/Ella/Ud. dice
Nosotros decimos
Vosotros decís
Ellos/Ellas/Uds. dicen

PRETERITE TENSE
Yo dije
Tú dijiste
Él/Ella/Ud. dijo
Nosotros dijimos
Vosotros dijisteis
Ellos/Ellas/Uds. dijeron

DECIR

THE PRESENT TENSE	THE PRETERITE TENSE
Yo _____ la verdad.	Ellos _____ que el examen es hoy.
Ella no _____ nada importante.	¿Qué _____ tú al profesor?
Nosotros _____ hola a las personas.	Ud. _____ que ella es simpática.
¿ _____ ellos que soy malo?	Nosotros _____ adiós al empleado.
Tú _____ que mañana va a llover.	Yo no _____ una mentira.

DEJAR
to leave behind

deh-hahr

KEYWORD:
dee jay…_leaves behind_
dejar

The **dee jay _leaves behind_** his hairspray

PRESENT TENSE

Yo dejo

Tú dejas

Él/Ella/Ud. deja

Nosotros dejamos

Vosotros dejáis

Ellos/Ellas/Uds. dejan

PRETERITE TENSE

Yo dejé

Tú dejaste

Él/Ella/Ud. dejó

Nosotros dejamos

Vosotros dejasteis

Ellos/Ellas/Uds. dejaron

DEJAR

THE PRESENT TENSE	THE PRETERITE TENSE
Tú _____ la bolsa en la mesa.	Yo no _____ la cámara en el coche.
Nosotros _____ los zapatos en el armario.	Ellos _____ las direcciones en la casa.
Yo no _____ la comida en mi plato.	Ud. no _____ la calculadora en la clase.
¿ _____ ellos las fotos en el suelo?	¿ _____ tú la puerta abierta?
Ella _____ las monedas por la casa.	¿Dónde _____ Ana las toallas?

DESCANSAR

dehs-kahn-sahr

to rest

KEYWORD:
desk...**_rests_**
descansar

Wes **_rests_** on his **des**k

PRESENT TENSE

Yo descanso

Tú descansas

Él/Ella/Ud. descansa

Nosotros descansamos

Vosotros descansáis

Ellos/Ellas/Uds. descansan

PRETERITE TENSE

Yo descansé

Tú descansaste

Él/Ella/Ud. descansó

Nosotros descansamos

Vosotros descansasteis

Ellos/Ellas/Uds. descansaron

DESCANSAR

THE PRESENT TENSE	THE PRETERITE TENSE
Ella _____ en una hamaca.	Ella no _____ anoche.
Nosotros no _____ por la mañana.	Uds. _____ en la sala.
Tú _____ en la clase.	¿Cuándo _____ tú?
¿Dónde _____ ellos después del día?	Yo _____ toda la mañana.
Yo no _____ en mi casa.	Elena no _____ antes de cocinar.

DESPERTARSE

dehs-pehr-**tahr**-seh

to wake up

KEYWORD:
desperately…_**wake up**_
despertarse

Andy **desper**ately tried to _**wake up**_ Mandy

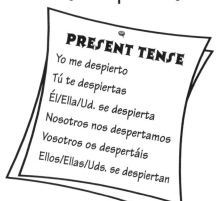

PRESENT TENSE

Yo me despierto

Tú te despiertas

Él/Ella/Ud. se despierta

Nosotros nos despertamos

Vosotros os despertáis

Ellos/Ellas/Uds. se despiertan

PRETERITE TENSE

Yo me desperté

Tú te despertaste

Él/Ella/Ud. se despertó

Nosotros nos despertamos

Vosotros os despertasteis

Ellos/Ellas/Uds. se despertaron

DESPERTARSE

THE PRESENT TENSE	THE PRETERITE TENSE
Yo _____ a las siete.	Ellas _____ temprano esta mañana.
Ella no _____ temprano.	Tú _____ antes de las siete.
Tú _____ antes que los demás.	¿Cuándo _____ Juan?
¿A qué hora _____ Marco?	Yo no _____ tarde ayer.
Uds. _____ antes que yo.	Nosotros _____ tarde los domingos.

DORMIR
to sleep

dohr-meer

KEYWORD:
dorm...*sleeps*
dormir

Norm *sleeps* in the **dorm**

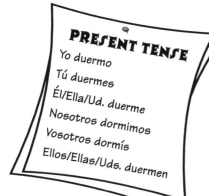

PRESENT TENSE

Yo duermo

Tú duermes

Él/Ella/Ud. duerme

Nosotros dormimos

Vosotros dormís

Ellos/Ellas/Uds. duermen

PRETERITE TENSE

Yo dormí

Tú dormiste

Él/Ella/Ud. durmió

Nosotros dormimos

Vosotros dormisteis

Ellos/Ellas/Uds. durmieron

DORMIR

THE PRESENT TENSE	THE PRETERITE TENSE
Yo _____ mucho.	Ella no _____ nada anoche.
Ellos no _____ nada los fines de semana.	
Uds. _____ ocho horas cada noche.	Tú no _____ en la cama.
¿ _____ tú con los niños?	¿ _____ Uds. bien?
Nosotros _____ muy poco en mi casa.	Yo _____ en el sofá.
	Nosotros _____ con los perros.

DURAR
to last

doo-rahr

KEYWORD:
durable...**last**
durar

2000 BC

1995

Durable things **last** forever

PRESENT TENSE

Yo duro

Tú duras

Él/Ella/Ud. dura

Nosotros duramos

Vosotros duráis

Ellos/Ellas/Uds. duran

PRETERITE TENSE

Yo duré

Tú duraste

Él/Ella/Ud. duró

Nosotros duramos

Vosotros durasteis

Ellos/Ellas/Uds. duraron

DURAR

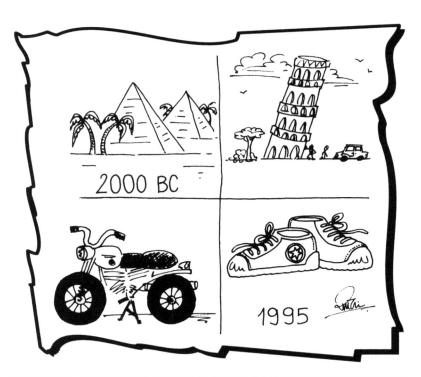

2000 BC

1995

THE PRESENT TENSE	THE PRETERITE TENSE
El concierto _____ mucho tiempo.	Mario _____ hasta las seis.
Nosotros _____ poco cuando corremos.	Los niños no _____ ni cinco minutos.
Ud. no _____ hasta el final.	Uds. _____ más que yo.
Los hermanos _____ cinco horas.	La clase _____ hasta muy tarde
Yo _____ hasta que el timbre suena.	Yo no _____ toda la noche.

ENCONTRAR

to find

*ehn-kohn-**trahr***

KEYWORD:
encounter...**_find_**
encontrar

Encounter...to **_find_**..it's all the same in my mind!

PRESENT TENSE

Yo encuentro

Tú encuentras

Él/Ella/Ud. encuentra

Nosotros encontramos

Vosotros encontráis

Ellos/Ellas/Uds. encuentran

PRETERITE TENSE

Yo encontré

Tú encontraste

Él/Ella/Ud. encontró

Nosotros encontramos

Vosotros encontrasteis

Ellos/Ellas/Uds. encontraron

ENCONTRAR

THE PRESENT TENSE	THE PRETERITE TENSE
Ellos _____ las llaves en la calle.	Yo no _____ la calle.
Nosotros _____ la respuesta en la lectura.	Nosotros _____ la pizzería.
¿ _____ ella la información?	Tú _____ tu cartera.
Yo no _____ lo que busco.	¿ _____ Elena su bolso?
Tú _____ el número de teléfono.	Ellas no _____ la fiesta.

ENFERMARSE

*en-fehr-**mahr**-seh*

to get sick

KEYWORD:
infirmary...***get sick***
enfermarse

When you **_get sick_**, get to the **infirmar**y quick

PRESENT TENSE
Yo me enfermo
Tú te enfermas
Él/Ella/Ud. se enferma
Nosotros nos enfermamos
Vosotros os enfermáis
Ellos/Ellas/Uds. se enferman

PRETERITE TENSE
Yo me enfermé
Tú te enfermaste
Él/Ella/Ud. se enfermó
Nosotros nos enfermamos
Vosotros os enfermasteis
Ellos/Ellas/Uds. se enfermaron

ENFERMARSE

THE PRESENT TENSE	THE PRETERITE TENSE
Yo no _____ frecuentemente.	Él _____ cuando estudió toda la noche.
Ella _____ cuando trabaja mucho.	Ellas no _____ en Alaska.
Nosotros _____ cada invierno.	Yo _____ tres veces en un mes.
¿ _____ tú mientras trabajas?	¿ _____ Ud. después de comer?
Ellos _____ cuando esquían.	Tú no _____ en mi casa.

ESCRIBIR
to write

ehs-kree-beer

KEYWORD:
scribbles…___writes___
escribir

Mike **scrib**bles when he ___writes___

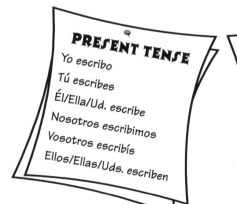

PRESENT TENSE

Yo escribo

Tú escribes

Él/Ella/Ud. escribe

Nosotros escribimos

Vosotros escribís

Ellos/Ellas/Uds. escriben

PRETERITE TENSE

Yo escribí

Tú escribiste

Él/Ella/Ud. escribió

Nosotros escribimos

Vosotros escribisteis

Ellos/Ellas/Uds. escribieron

ESCRIBIR

THE PRESENT TENSE	THE PRETERITE TENSE
Nosotros _____ muchas cartas.	Ellas no _____ a sus amigas.
Yo _____ a mi madre.	Yo _____ la nota.
Ellos no _____ a nadie.	¿ _____ Maria las instrucciones?
¿ _____ tú una carta a tu familia?	Él no _____ el nombre de la profesora.
Él no _____ el libro.	Nosotros _____ las letras en la pizarra.

ESCUCHAR

to listen to

ehs-kou-*chahr*

KEYWORD:
*escu*ses...**listen to**
escuchar

On board: Detention for those with no homework... NO ESCUSES

Ms. Chuses doesn't **listen to** *escu*ses

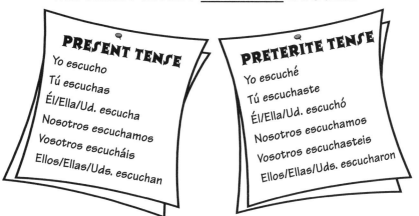

PRESENT TENSE
Yo escucho
Tú escuchas
Él/Ella/Ud. escucha
Nosotros escuchamos
Vosotros escucháis
Ellos/Ellas/Uds. escuchan

PRETERITE TENSE
Yo escuché
Tú escuchaste
Él/Ella/Ud. escuchó
Nosotros escuchamos
Vosotros escuchasteis
Ellos/Ellas/Uds. escucharon

ESCUCHAR

THE PRESENT TENSE	THE PRETERITE TENSE
Ella _____ música durante el día.	¿ _____ ellos las noticias?
Yo no _____ música clásica.	Yo no _____ nada anoche.
Nosotros _____ el ruido por la ventana.	Ella _____ al niño.
Uds. _____ las palabras del presidente.	Nosotros _____ los mandatos del jefe.
¿ _____ tú la television?	Tú _____ el anuncio.

ESPERAR
to wait for

ehs-peh-rahr

KEYWORD:
*esp*ress...**waits for**
esperar

LOCAL TRAIN HERE ⬇

ESPRESS TRAIN HERE ⬇

Only Mr. Lane **waits for** the **esp**ress train

PRESENT TENSE
Yo espero
Tú esperas
Él/Ella/Ud. espera
Nosotros esperamos
Vosotros esperáis
Ellos/Ellas/Uds. esperan

PRETERITE TENSE
Yo esperé
Tú esperaste
Él/Ella/Ud. esperó
Nosotros esperamos
Vosotros esperasteis
Ellos/Ellas/Uds. esperaron

ESPERAR

THE PRESENT TENSE	THE PRETERITE TENSE
Ella _____ el autobús.	Él _____ dos horas anoche.
Yo no _____ las noticias.	¿ _____ tú un café?
Tú _____ ir a la iglesia.	Yo _____ el tren ayer.
¿ _____ ellos una llamada?	Pablo _____ recibir el dinero.
Nosotros _____ una respuesta.	Los campesinos _____ la lluvia.

ESTUDIAR

to study

ehs-too-dee-yahr

KEYWORD:
students...**study**
estudiar

The **stud**ents **study** with their buddies

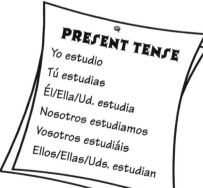

PRESENT TENSE

Yo estudio
Tú estudias
Él/Ella/Ud. estudia
Nosotros estudiamos
Vosotros estudiáis
Ellos/Ellas/Uds. estudian

PRETERITE TENSE

Yo estudié
Tú estudiaste
Él/Ella/Ud. estudió
Nosotros estudiamos
Vosotros estudiasteis
Ellos/Ellas/Uds. estudiaron

ESTUDIAR

THE PRESENT TENSE	THE PRETERITE TENSE
Nosotros _____ juntos.	Yo no _____ anoche.
Tú no _____ mucho.	Cada mañana ella _____ los verbos.
¿ _____ él con su amigo?	Nosotros no _____ en la biblioteca.
Yo _____ todos los días.	Los amigos _____ después de la escuela.
Ellos _____ los domingos.	¿ _____ tú para el examen?

EVITAR
to avoid

eh-vee-**tahr**

KEYWORD:
vitamins…***avoid***
evitar

The twins ***avoid*** their **vita**mins

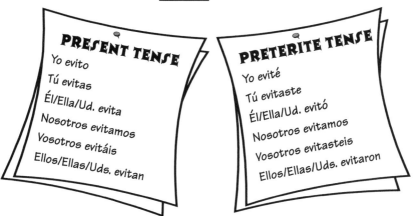

PRESENT TENSE
Yo evito
Tú evitas
Él/Ella/Ud. evita
Nosotros evitamos
Vosotros evitáis
Ellos/Ellas/Uds. evitan

PRETERITE TENSE
Yo evité
Tú evitaste
Él/Ella/Ud. evitó
Nosotros evitamos
Vosotros evitasteis
Ellos/Ellas/Uds. evitaron

EVITAR

THE PRESENT TENSE	THE PRETERITE TENSE
Ellos _____ el problema.	Ella _____ el cuarto oscuro.
Tú _____ la situación.	Nosotros _____ la sala grande.
Nosotros _____ las grasas.	El gato _____ la fiesta.
¿ _____ ella la televisión?	¿ _____ tú la oficina del director?
Yo _____ los dulces.	Yo _____ ir al concierto.

FUMAR
to smoke

KEYWORD:
fum*es*...**_smoking_**
fumar

The **fum**es from his **_smoking_** cause choking

PRESENT TENSE
Yo fumo
Tú fumas
Él/Ella/Ud. fuma
Nosotros fumamos
Vosotros fumáis
Ellos/Ellas/Uds. fuman

PRETERITE TENSE
Yo fumé
Tú fumaste
Él/Ella/Ud. fumó
Nosotros fumamos
Vosotros fumasteis
Ellos/Ellas/Uds. fumaron

FUMAR

THE PRESENT TENSE	THE PRETERITE TENSE
Ellos no _____ nunca.	Ella _____ tres veces ayer.
Yo no _____ los fines de semana.	Tú no _____ durante la clase.
Él _____ cuando está en una fiesta.	Yo _____ detrás del edificio.
¿ _____ tú con los amigos?	Paco _____ una vez en la vida.
Nosotros _____ los cigarros.	Mis tíos _____ una pipa.

GANAR
to win

gah-nahr

KEYWORD:
gangster...**_wins_**
ganar

THE WINNER

The **gan**gster **_wins_** a hamster

PRESENT TENSE

Yo gano

Tú ganas

Él/Ella/Ud. gana

Nosotros ganamos

Vosotros ganáis

Ellos/Ellas/Uds. ganan

PRETERITE TENSE

Yo gané

Tú ganaste

Él/Ella/Ud. ganó

Nosotros ganamos

Vosotros ganasteis

Ellos/Ellas/Uds. ganaron

GANAR

THE PRESENT TENSE	THE PRETERITE TENSE
Tú _____ el premio.	Él _____ el campeonato.
Nosotros no _____ el regalo.	Uds. no _____ porque llegaron tarde.
Yo _____ porque practico mucho.	Nosotros _____ el coche nuevo.
Ellos _____ en el sorteo.	Yo _____ un osito de peluche.
¿ _____ ella la beca al extranjero?	¿ _____ ellos la medalla de oro?

GASTAR
to spend

gahs-tahr

KEYWORD:
gas...<u>*spends*</u>
gastar

Mama Cass **<u>spends</u>** too much on **gas**

PRESENT TENSE
Yo gasto
Tú gastas
Él/Ella/Ud. gasta
Nosotros gastamos
Vosotros gastáis
Ellos/Ellas/Uds. gastan

PRETERITE TENSE
Yo gasté
Tú gastaste
Él/Ella/Ud. gastó
Nosotros gastamos
Vosotros gastasteis
Ellos/Ellas/Uds. gastaron

GASTAR

THE PRESENT TENSE	THE PRETERITE TENSE
Ellas _____ mucho dinero.	¿En qué _____ tú el dinero?
Tú no _____ todo en un día.	Ella _____ todo en el parque de atracciones.
Nosotros _____ el salario en el supermercado.	Nosotros _____ la mitad en Las Vegas.
¿ _____ él su sueldo en ropa?	Los profesores _____ su tiempo repasando la lección.
Yo _____ muy poco.	Yo _____ mi tiempo estudiando.

GRITAR
to shout

gree-tahr

AOAOAA

KEYWORD:
grit**s**...*shouts*
gritar

GRITS!

Mama ***shouts*** "**Grit**s!" to the nitwits

PRESENT TENSE
Yo grito
Tú gritas
Él/Ella/Ud. grita
Nosotros gritamos
Vosotros gritáis
Ellos/Ellas/Uds. gritan

PRETERITE TENSE
Yo grité
Tú gritaste
Él/Ella/Ud. gritó
Nosotros gritamos
Vosotros gritasteis
Ellos/Ellas/Uds. gritaron

GRITAR

THE PRESENT TENSE	THE PRETERITE TENSE
Yo no _____ a mis hijos.	Él _____ cuando vio el coche nuevo.
Ellos _____ cuando están enfadados.	Yo _____ a los ladrones que robaron mi casa.
Tú _____ cada mañana.	Nosotros _____ cuando vimos el precio.
Nosotros no _____ si no hay problemas.	¿ _____ ellos ayer en la fiesta?
¿ _____ ella a sus estudiantes?	Mi compañero _____ cuando el conductor frenó.

HABLAR
to speak

KEYWORD:
bla..bla..bla...*speaking*
hablar

Bla..bla..bla...stop ***speaking*** like your ma!

PRESENT TENSE
Yo hablo

Tú hablas

Él/Ella/Ud. habla

Nosotros hablamos

Vosotros habláis

Ellos/Ellas/Uds. hablan

PRETERITE TENSE
Yo hablé

Tú hablaste

Él/Ella/Ud. habló

Nosotros hablamos

Vosotros hablasteis

Ellos/Ellas/Uds. hablaron

HABLAR

THE PRESENT TENSE	THE PRETERITE TENSE
Tú no _____ inglés bien.	Ella no _____ con Esteban ayer.
Ellos _____ todos los días.	¿ _____ tú con la policía?
Yo _____ cinco idiomas.	Ana y yo _____ con los padres.
¿ _____ Ud. español?	¿ _____ Uds. con los estudiantes?
Nosotros _____ poco por la mañana.	Yo _____ con los vecinos.

HACER
to do, make

ah-sehr

KEYWORD:
hackers...**_do_**
hacer

Computer **hac**kers **_do_**... bad things to me and you

PRESENT TENSE
Yo hago
Tú haces
Él/Ella/Ud. hace
Nosotros hacemos
Vosotros hacéis
Ellos/Ellas/Uds. hacen

PRETERITE TENSE
Yo hice
Tú hiciste
Él/Ella/Ud. hizo
Nosotros hicimos
Vosotros hicisteis
Ellos/Ellas/Uds. hicieron

HACER

THE PRESENT TENSE	THE PRETERITE TENSE
Ellas no _____ la tarea.	Él no _____ nada para ayudar.
Yo no _____ los planes para la clase.	Uds. _____ mucho el día de la boda.
Nosotros _____ el pan para la fiesta.	Nosotros _____ la presentación ayer.
¿ _____ tú una visita al hospital?	¿ _____ Pepe el flan para la fiesta?
Ud. no _____ el proyecto.	Yo _____ todo lo posible.

IR
to go

eer

KEYWORD:
Virgos…**_goes_**
ir

Everyone **_goes_** to Virgos

PRESENT TENSE

Yo voy

Tú vas

Él/Ella/Ud. va

Nosotros vamos

Vosotros vais

Ellos/Ellas/Uds. van

PRETERITE TENSE

Yo fui

Tú fuiste

Él/Ella/Ud. fue

Nosotros fuimos

Vosotros fuisteis

Ellos/Ellas/Uds. fueron

IR

THE PRESENT TENSE	THE PRETERITE TENSE
Tú _____ a la playa con Miguel.	¿Adónde _____ tú anoche?
Ellos no _____ conmigo hoy.	Ellos _____ con sus padres.
¿ _____ él a la biblioteca?	Yo no _____ a casa.
Yo no _____ muy temprano.	El equipo _____ al campeonato.
Nosotros _____ todos los veranos.	Los perros _____ al bosque.

JUGAR
to play

hoo-gahr

KEYWORD:
juggles...**play**
jugar

While others **play**, Pablo **jug**gles away

PRESENT TENSE
Yo juego
Tú juegas
Él/Ella/Ud. juega
Nosotros jugamos
Vosotros jugáis
Ellos/Ellas/Uds. juegan

PRETERITE TENSE
Yo jugué
Tú jugaste
Él/Ella/Ud. jugó
Nosotros jugamos
Vosotros jugasteis
Ellos/Ellas/Uds. jugaron

JUGAR

THE PRESENT TENSE	THE PRETERITE TENSE
Nosotros no _____ al béisbol.	Él _____ ayer con el equipo.
Yo _____ todos los días.	Tú _____ a las cartas.
Ella no _____ hoy.	¿Por qué no _____ Antonio en el partido?
¿ _____ tú esta tarde?	Yo no _____ anoche.
Ellos no _____ porque no tienen tiempo.	Nosotros _____ en el parque.

LAVARSE
to wash

(lah-**bahr**-seh)

Corey **washes** up in the **lava**tory

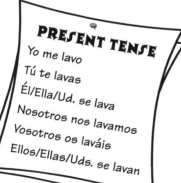

PRESENT TENSE

Yo me lavo
Tú te lavas
Él/Ella/Ud. se lava
Nosotros nos lavamos
Vosotros os laváis
Ellos/Ellas/Uds. se lavan

PRETERITE TENSE

Yo me lavé
Tú te lavaste
Él/Ella/Ud. se lavó
Nosotros nos lavamos
Vosotros os lavasteis
Ellos/Ellas/Uds. se lavaron

LAVARSE

THE PRESENT TENSE	THE PRETERITE TENSE
Ellos _____ antes de comer.	Uds. _____ la cara en la bañera.
Tú _____ los dientes.	Él no _____ bien anoche.
Nosotros _____ el pelo.	Yo no _____ ayer.
¿ _____ ella las manos?	¿Cuándo _____ tú los pies?
Yo _____ cuando estoy sucio.	Los gatos _____ en el agua.

LEER
to read

leh-ehr

KEYWORD:
lee...*reads*
leer

Lee *reads* more than me

PRESENT TENSE

Yo leo

Tú lees

Él/Ella/Ud. lee

Nosotros leemos

Vosotros leéis

Ellos/Ellas/Uds. leen

PRETERITE TENSE

Yo leí

Tú leíste

Él/Ella/Ud. leyó

Nosotros leímos

Vosotros leísteis

Ellos/Ellas/Uds. leyeron

LEER

THE PRESENT TENSE	THE PRETERITE TENSE
Ella _____ todas las noches.	Ellos _____ el anuncio en la puerta.
Nosotros _____ los libros cómicos.	Yo no _____ el periódico esta mañana.
¿ _____ ellos los cuentos?	Nosotros _____ lo que pasó.
Tú no _____ mucho.	¿Cuándo _____ tú el artículo?
Yo _____ cada mañana.	Los niños no _____ la tarea bien.

LEVANTARSE

to get up

KEYWORD:
lev*i*tating...***Get up***
levantarse

No waiting! ***Get up*** by **lev**itating!

PRESENT TENSE

Yo me levanto
Tú te levantas
Él/Ella/Ud. se levanta
Nosotros nos levantamos
Vosotros os levantáis
Ellos/Ellas/Uds. se levantan

PRETERITE TENSE

Yo me levanté
Tú te levantaste
Él/Ella/Ud. se levantó
Nosotros nos levantamos
Vosotros os levantasteis
Ellos/Ellas/Uds. se levantaron

LEVANTARSE

THE PRESENT TENSE	THE PRETERITE TENSE
Yo _____ a las siete cada mañana.	Ella no _____ para ir a la playa.
Ellos no _____ tarde.	Nosotros _____ antes que los demás.
Él _____ con sus hijos.	¿Cuándo _____ Mario el domingo?
Nosotros no _____ a tiempo.	Yo no _____ porque tenía sueño.
¿ _____ tú temprano los fines de semana?	Los perros _____ con las gallinas.

LIMPIAR
to clean

lihm-pih-**ahr**

KEYWORD:
limousine...**cleans**
limpiar

Gene **cleans** the **lim**ousine.

PRESENT TENSE
Yo limpio
Tú limpias
Él/Ella/Ud. limpia
Nosotros limpiamos
Vosotros limpiáis
Ellos/Ellas/Uds. limpian

PRETERITE TENSE
Yo limpié
Tú limpiaste
Él/Ella/Ud. limpió
Nosotros limpiamos
Vosotros limpiasteis
Ellos/Ellas/Uds. limpiaron

LIMPIAR

THE PRESENT TENSE	THE PRETERITE TENSE
Uds. no _____ el coche.	Yo no _____ nada en la casa ayer.
Yo _____ mi cuarto.	Ella siempre _____ la cocina primero.
Tú _____ la casa.	¿ _____ tú los platos?
Nosotros _____ las ventanas.	Nosotros _____ la ropa después del partido.
¿ _____ Ud. los baños?	Ellos no _____ las gafas anoche.

LLAMAR
to call

yah-*mahr*

KEYWORD:
llama...*calls*
llamar

The **llama *calls*** his mama

PRESENT TENSE
Yo llamo
Tú llamas
Él/Ella/Ud. llama
Nosotros llamamos
Vosotros llamáis
Ellos/Ellas/Uds. llaman

PRETERITE TENSE
Yo llamé
Tú llamaste
Él/Ella/Ud. llamó
Nosotros llamamos
Vosotros llamasteis
Ellos/Ellas/Uds. llamaron

LLAMAR

THE PRESENT TENSE	THE PRETERITE TENSE
Yo _____ a la policía.	¿Por qué no _____ tú ayer?
Nosotros _____ el banco.	Uds. _____ la tienda anoche.
Ellos no _____ porque no tienen un teléfono.	Yo _____ a mi padre tres veces hoy.
¿ _____ tú la farmacia?	Pedro _____ a su novia por la mañana.
Ella no _____ a su familia nunca.	Mis amigos _____ mi casa esta mañana.

LLEGAR
to arrive

yeh-gahr

ARRIVALS

KEYWORD:
i**llega**l...*arrive*
llegar

It's i**llega**l to ***arrive*** at school with a beagle

PRESENT TENSE
Yo llego
Tú llegas
Él/Ella/Ud. llega
Nosotros llegamos
Vosotros llegáis
Ellos/Ellas/Uds. llegan

PRETERITE TENSE
Yo llegué
Tú llegaste
Él/Ella/Ud. llegó
Nosotros llegamos
Vosotros llegasteis
Ellos/Ellas/Uds. llegaron

LLEGAR

THE PRESENT TENSE	THE PRETERITE TENSE
Ellas _____ siempre a las cuatro.	Ud. _____ anoche.
Nosotros _____ en moto.	¿ _____ ellos en avión?
Yo _____ con mi prima.	Tú _____ a los dos.
¿ _____ tú con el regalo?	Nosotros _____ con el dinero.
Ella no _____ hasta que la fiesta empieza.	Yo _____ a las diez.

LLEVAR
to wear

yeh-vahr

KEYWORD:
levi's…*wear*
llevar

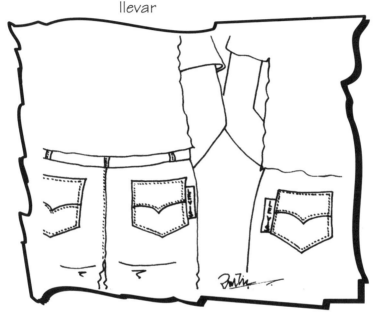

The guys *wear* Lev**i**'s®

PRESENT TENSE

Yo llevo

Tú llevas

Él/Ella/Ud. lleva

Nosotros llevamos

Vosotros lleváis

Ellos/Ellas/Uds. llevan

PRETERITE TENSE

Yo llevé

Tú llevaste

Él/Ella/Ud. llevó

Nosotros llevamos

Vosotros llevasteis

Ellos/Ellas/Uds. llevaron

LLEVAR

THE PRESENT TENSE	THE PRETERITE TENSE
Nosotros _____ los pantalones.	Él no _____ los pantalones de Miguel hoy.
Ella no _____ el vestido hoy.	Uds. _____ los guantes ayer.
Uds. _____ la misma chaqueta.	¿Cuándo _____ ellos el uniforme?
¿Por qué no _____ tú la camisa?	Yo no _____ el traje de vestir porque no me gusta.
Yo _____ la gorra de los Yankees.	María no _____ la falda anoche.

MANDAR
to send

mahn-**dahr**

KEYWORD:
man...*sends*
mandar

A **man** *<u>sends</u>* an email to Japan

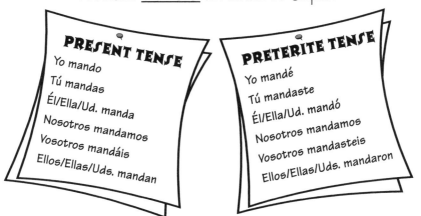

PRESENT TENSE
Yo mando

Tú mandas

Él/Ella/Ud. manda

Nosotros mandamos

Vosotros mandáis

Ellos/Ellas/Uds. mandan

PRETERITE TENSE
Yo mandé

Tú mandaste

Él/Ella/Ud. mandó

Nosotros mandamos

Vosotros mandasteis

Ellos/Ellas/Uds. mandaron

MANDAR

THE PRESENT TENSE	THE PRETERITE TENSE
Ella _____ la carta.	Mario _____ el certificado.
Nosotros _____ el paquete.	Los niños no _____ las fotos.
Ud. no _____ los zapatos.	Uds. _____ las invitaciones.
¿ _____ tú el regalo?	¿ _____ tú las entradas?
Yo _____ los papeles.	Yo no _____ el permiso.

METER

to put in

meh-tehr

KEYWORD:
meter...*puts in*
meter

Peter **_puts_** money **_in_** the **meter**

PRESENT TENSE

Yo meto

Tú metes

Él/Ella/Ud. mete

Nosotros metemos

Vosotros metéis

Ellos/Ellas/Uds. meten

PRETERITE TENSE

Yo metí

Tú metiste

Él/Ella/Ud. metió

Nosotros metimos

Vosotros metisteis

Ellos/Ellas/Uds. metieron

METER

THE PRESENT TENSE	THE PRETERITE TENSE
Ella _____ la ropa en el cajón.	Él _____ la mano en la masa.
Tú _____ el dinero en el bolsillo.	¿Cuándo _____ tú la cartera en mi bolso?
¿Por qué no _____ ella la carta en el sobre?	Yo no _____ los papeles en la chaqueta.
Yo _____ las monedas en la máquina.	Nosotros _____ la cabeza en el agujero.
Nosotros _____ las camisas en el lavaplatos.	Ana _____ el pie en arena.

MIRAR
to look at

mee-rahr

KEYWORD:
mirror…**_looks at_**
mirar

Roger **_looks at_** the **mir**ror

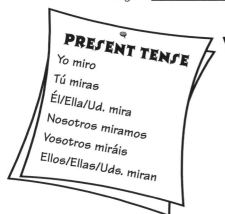

PRESENT TENSE
Yo miro
Tú miras
Él/Ella/Ud. mira
Nosotros miramos
Vosotros miráis
Ellos/Ellas/Uds. miran

PRETERITE TENSE
Yo miré
Tú miraste
Él/Ella/Ud. miró
Nosotros miramos
Vosotros mirasteis
Ellos/Ellas/Uds. miraron

MIRAR

THE PRESENT TENSE	THE PRETERITE TENSE
Ellos _____ la televisión.	Él no _____ por la ventana.
Yo _____ el partido.	Nosotros _____ el desfile.
¿ _____ ella los resultados?	Yo _____ porque fue divertido.
Tú no _____ las notas de la clase.	¿ _____ tú la película?
Uds. _____ las noticias todas las noches.	Las amigas _____ el nuevo video.

NADAR
to swim

nah-**dahr**

KEYWORD:
nada...**_swim_**mer
nadar

He's definitely **nada** _**swim**_mer

PRESENT TENSE
Yo nado
Tú nadas
Él/Ella/Ud. nada
Nosotros nadamos
Vosotros nadáis
Ellos/Ellas/Uds. nadan

PRETERITE TENSE
Yo nadé
Tú nadaste
Él/Ella/Ud. nadó
Nosotros nadamos
Vosotros nadasteis
Ellos/Ellas/Uds. nadaron

NADAR

THE PRESENT TENSE	THE PRETERITE TENSE
Yo _____ todos los días.	Ellos no _____ ayer.
Ellos no _____ en el mar.	Nosotros _____ con el bebé.
Nosotros _____ cuando hace buen tiempo.	Tú _____ con tus amigos.
Uds. _____ por la mañana.	¿Por qué no _____ ella con nosotros?
¿Cuándo _____ ella en la piscina?	Yo _____ cada mañana a las siete.

ODIAR
to hate

oh-dee-**ahr**

KEYWORD:
odor...**hate**
odiar

I **hate** body **od**or

PRESENT TENSE
Yo odio
Tú odias
Él/Ella/Ud. odia
Nosotros odiamos
Vosotros odiáis
Ellos/Ellas/Uds. odian

PRETERITE TENSE
Yo odié
Tú odiaste
Él/Ella/Ud. odió
Nosotros odiamos
Vosotros odiasteis
Ellos/Ellas/Uds. odiaron

ODIAR

THE PRESENT TENSE	THE PRETERITE TENSE
Yo _____ el color azul.	El año pasado, él _____ el beísbol.
Nosotros _____ la ópera.	Nosotros _____ la tarea.
Ella _____ los bailes.	Ellos _____ los deportes.
Tú _____ los vegetales.	¿Por qué _____ tú a tu vecino?
¿Por qué _____ ella el coche nuevo?	Rosa no _____ al profesor.

OÍR
to hear

oh-eer

KEYWORD:
oír...*hear*
oír

I *hear* oh-ear....**oír...oír**

PRESENT TENSE
Yo oigo
Tú oyes
Él/Ella/Ud. oye
Nosotros oímos
Vosotros oís
Ellos/Ellas/Uds. oyen

PRETERITE TENSE
Yo oí
Tú oíste
Él/Ella/Ud. oyó
Nosotros oímos
Vosotros oísteis
Ellos/Ellas/Uds. oyeron

OÍR

THE PRESENT TENSE	THE PRETERITE TENSE
Uds. _____ la música.	¿Qué _____ Ud. del accidente?
Nosotros no _____ nada en la radio.	Ellos _____ lo que pasó.
¿ _____ tú el partido?	Tú no _____ lo peor de todo.
Yo _____ todo en mi cuarto.	¿ _____ Uds. que mañana Elena se va a casar?
Ella no _____ la televisión.	Yo _____ que el examen es difícil.

PAGAR
to pay

pah-gahr

KEYWORD:
page…**pays**
pagar

Kirk **pays** for a **pag**e of homework

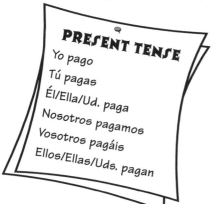

PRESENT TENSE

Yo pago
Tú pagas
Él/Ella/Ud. paga
Nosotros pagamos
Vosotros pagáis
Ellos/Ellas/Uds. pagan

PRETERITE TENSE

Yo pagué
Tú pagaste
Él/Ella/Ud. pagó
Nosotros pagamos
Vosotros pagasteis
Ellos/Ellas/Uds. pagaron

PAGAR

THE PRESENT TENSE	THE PRETERITE TENSE
Ella _____ la comida.	Mario _____ el billete.
Nosotros _____ en el banco.	Los niños no _____ los dulces.
Ana no _____ los zapatos.	Ud. _____ con tarjeta.
¿ _____ tú a Juan?	¿ _____ ellas las entradas?
Yo _____ a mi padre.	Yo no _____ la factura.

PARAR
to stop

pah-*rahr*

KEYWORD:
parade...**_stops_**
parar

The **para**de **_stops_** for lemonade

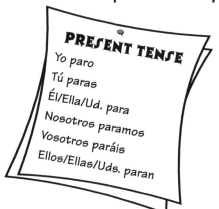

PRESENT TENSE

Yo paro

Tú paras

Él/Ella/Ud. para

Nosotros paramos

Vosotros paráis

Ellos/Ellas/Uds. paran

PRETERITE TENSE

Yo paré

Tú paraste

Él/Ella/Ud. paró

Nosotros paramos

Vosotros parasteis

Ellos/Ellas/Uds. pararon

PARAR

THE PRESENT TENSE	THE PRETERITE TENSE
Ellos _____ el autobús.	Ella _____ en Boston ayer.
Yo _____ la música.	Nosotros no _____ el coche durante el viaje.
Nosotros _____ para hablar con la policía.	Yo _____ para ver el accidente.
¿ _____ Ud. en el supermercado?	Tú _____ de fumar el año pasado..
Tú no _____ nunca.	¿ _____ él la moto en la calle?

PEDIR
to ask for

peh-**deer**

KEYWORD:
pediatrician...**_asks for_**
pedir

PEDIATRICIAN'S OFFICE

PLEASE...

The **pedi**atrician **_asks for_** permission

PRESENT TENSE

Yo pido

Tú pides

Él/Ella/Ud. pide

Nosotros pedimos

Vosotros pedís

Ellos/Ellas/Uds. piden

PRETERITE TENSE

Yo pedí

Tú pediste

Él/Ella/Ud. pidió

Nosotros pedimos

Vosotros pedisteis

Ellos/Ellas/Uds. pidieron

PEDIR

THE PRESENT TENSE	THE PRETERITE TENSE
Tú _____ mucho.	Ellos _____ una pizza.
Ella no _____ nada cuando está con su novio.	¿Qué _____ María?
Nosotros _____ el menú.	Yo no _____ el especial de la casa.
Yo _____ lo mismo siempre.	Él _____ la ensalada con aceite.
Uds. no _____ las hamburguesas.	Nosotros _____ las llaves de la casa.

PEGAR
to hit

peh-gahr

KEYWORD:
Peggy...**hits**
pegar

Peggy Sue **hits** harder than you.

PRESENT TENSE
Yo pego
Tú pegas
Él/Ella/Ud. pega
Nosotros pegamos
Vosotros pegáis
Ellos/Ellas/Uds. pegan

PRETERITE TENSE
Yo pegué
Tú pegaste
Él/Ella/Ud. pegó
Nosotros pegamos
Vosotros pegasteis
Ellos/Ellas/Uds. pegaron

PEGAR

THE PRESENT TENSE	THE PRETERITE TENSE
Tú _____ a tus hermanos.	Yo no _____ a mi amigo ayer.
Ellos _____ la pared.	Él no _____ el balón.
Yo no _____ la pelota.	Uds. _____ los colchones.
¿ _____ ella su coche?	¿Por qué _____ tú la mesa?
Nosotros _____ el juguete.	Nosotros no _____ nada.

PENSAR
to think

pehn-sahr

KEYWORD:
Pensive…**_think_**
pensar

THINK TANK FOR PENSIVE PEOPLE

Pensive people **_think_** a lot

PRESENT TENSE
Yo pienso
Tú piensas
Él/Ella/Ud. piensa
Nosotros pensamos
Vosotros pensáis
Ellos/Ellas/Uds. piensan

PRETERITE TENSE
Yo pensé
Tú pensaste
Él/Ella/Ud. pensó
Nosotros pensamos
Vosotros pensasteis
Ellos/Ellas/Uds. pensaron

PENSAR

THINK TANK FOR PENSIVE PEOPLE

THE PRESENT TENSE	THE PRETERITE TENSE
Ella _____ que va a llover mañana.	Yo _____ que el reloj era de Juan.
Yo _____ que él es inteligente.	Nosotros _____ que el coche valía más dinero.
Nosotros _____ que la casa es cara.	Tú _____ que Ana era la esposa de Julio.
¿Qué _____ ellos de la idea?	¿Qué _____ ellas de mi proyecto?
Tú _____ que yo no sé nada.	Antonio _____ que fue muy interesante.

PERDER
to lose

KEYWORD:
perfect...**_lose_**
perder

Even Kings **_lose_** things because nobody is **per**fect

PRESENT TENSE
Yo pierdo
Tú pierdes
Él/Ella/Ud. pierde
Nosotros perdemos
Vosotros perdéis
Ellos/Ellas/Uds. pierden

PRETERITE TENSE
Yo perdí
Tú perdiste
Él/Ella/Ud. perdió
Nosotros perdimos
Vosotros perdisteis
Ellos/Ellas/Uds. perdieron

PERDER

THE PRESENT TENSE	THE PRETERITE TENSE
Nosotros _____ las llaves todos los días.	Tú _____ la mente.
Yo no _____ los examenes.	Yo _____ las direcciones de la fiesta.
Ellos _____ el coche cada día.	¿ _____ ellos el coche?
¿ _____ Ud. el control de la clase?	Nosotros _____ los pasteles.
Ella _____ su bolso en el museo.	Los perros _____ los huesos.

PONER
to put

KEYWORD:
poncho...**puts**
poner

Joe **puts** the **pon**cho on the snow

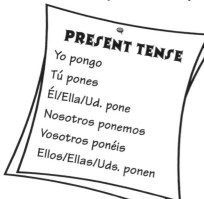

PRESENT TENSE
Yo pongo
Tú pones
Él/Ella/Ud. pone
Nosotros ponemos
Vosotros ponéis
Ellos/Ellas/Uds. ponen

PRETERITE TENSE
Yo puse
Tú pusiste
Él/Ella/Ud. puso
Nosotros pusimos
Vosotros pusisteis
Ellos/Ellas/Uds. pusieron

PONER

THE PRESENT TENSE	THE PRETERITE TENSE
Ella _____ el vaso en la mesa.	Antonio _____ la nota en el cajón.
Nosotros _____ las llaves en la chaqueta.	Los niños _____ los guantes en el suelo.
Juan no _____ los zapatos en el armario.	Yo _____ la radio en la cocina.
¿Dónde _____ tú el número?	¿ _____ ellas la manta en la cama?
Yo _____ los papeles en la basura.	Ud. no _____ el reloj en la caja.

PREGUNTAR

preh-goon-tahr

to ask

KEYWORD:
pregnant…***ask***
preguntar

Pregnant women ***ask*** more questions

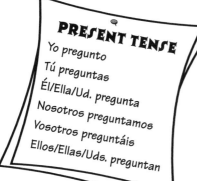

PRESENT TENSE

Yo pregunto
Tú preguntas
Él/Ella/Ud. pregunta
Nosotros preguntamos
Vosotros preguntáis
Ellos/Ellas/Uds. preguntan

PRETERITE TENSE

Yo pregunté
Tú preguntaste
Él/Ella/Ud. preguntó
Nosotros preguntamos
Vosotros preguntasteis
Ellos/Ellas/Uds. preguntaron

PREGUNTAR

THE PRESENT TENSE	THE PRETERITE TENSE
Él _____ por las niñas.	Ellas no _____ demasiado.
Yo no _____ qué hora es.	Ud. _____ dónde estaban los padres.
¿ _____ ellos por qué hay mucho tráfico?	¿ _____ tú a la policía?
¿Tú _____ por mí?	Él _____ por qué ellos no fueron a la iglesia.
Nosotros _____ cuándo ella vuelve.	Yo no _____ al empleado cuánto cuesta la computadora.

PROMETER

(proh-meh-tehr)

to promise

KEYWORD:
prom…*promises*
prometer

The **prom** **_promises_** to be the bomb

PRESENT TENSE

Yo prometo

Tú prometes

Él/Ella/Ud. promete

Nosotros prometemos

Vosotros prometéis

Ellos/Ellas/Uds. prometen

PRETERITE TENSE

Yo prometí

Tú prometiste

Él/Ella/Ud. prometió

Nosotros prometimos

Vosotros prometisteis

Ellos/Ellas/Uds. prometieron

PROMETER

THE PRESENT TENSE	THE PRETERITE TENSE
Ellos _____ hacer la tarea a tiempo.	Él _____ volver a las siete.
Yo no _____ donar más de $100.	Ud. _____ formar un grupo de cinco personas.
Tú _____ ser mi amigo.	¿Qué _____ tú hacer para el desfile?
¿Por qué _____ ella ir a Florida con Pablo?	Nosotros _____ ayudar en el jardín.
Nosotros _____ terminar el proyecto para mañana.	Yo no _____ estar con los niños todo el día.

QUERER
to want

keh-**rehr**

The **Que**en **_wants_** a driving machine

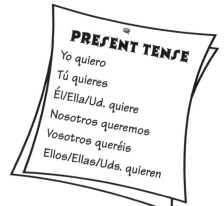

PRESENT TENSE

Yo quiero

Tú quieres

Él/Ella/Ud. quiere

Nosotros queremos

Vosotros queréis

Ellos/Ellas/Uds. quieren

PRETERITE TENSE

Yo quise

Tú quisiste

Él/Ella/Ud. quiso

Nosotros quisimos

Vosotros quisisteis

Ellos/Ellas/Uds. quisieron

QUERER

THE PRESENT TENSE	THE PRETERITE TENSE
Ella _____ su dinero hoy.	Ellas no _____ vender el coche.
Nosotros _____ mirar la televisión.	Nosotros no _____ entregar los papeles.
Yo no _____ viajar a España.	Yo _____ mudarme a Texas.
Ellos _____ ganar mucho dinero.	¿Por qué ella no _____ salir con José?
Uds. _____ trabajar en la computadora.	Tú no _____ verme ayer.

RECIBIR
to receive

rreh-see-beer

KEYWORD:
recipient…**_receives_**
recibir

This year's **reci**pient **_receives_** a compliment

PRESENT TENSE
Yo recibo

Tú recibes

Él/Ella/Ud. recibe

Nosotros recibimos

Vosotros recibís

Ellos/Ellas/Uds. reciben

PRETERITE TENSE
Yo recibí

Tú recibiste

Él/Ella/Ud. recibió

Nosotros recibimos

Vosotros recibisteis

Ellos/Ellas/Uds. recibieron

RECIBIR

THE PRESENT TENSE	THE PRETERITE TENSE
Tú _____ mucho dinero.	Ud. _____ el cheque la semana pasada.
Él _____ la llamada de su madre.	Yo no _____ nada de la oficina.
Nosotros _____ mucha ropa de nuestros amigos.	¿Qué _____ tú para la boda?
¿Qué _____ ellos en el correo?	Nosotros _____ una casa nueva.
Yo no _____ nada de nadie.	Ellos no _____ los regalos de sus abuelos.

RECORDAR

to remember

KEYWORD:
record...**_remember_**
recordar

Flo doesn't **_remember_** how to **record** her show

PRESENT TENSE

Yo recuerdo

Tú recuerdas

Él/Ella/Ud. recuerda

Nosotros recordamos

Vosotros recordáis

Ellos/Ellas/Uds. recuerdan

PRETERITE TENSE

Yo recordé

Tú recordaste

Él/Ella/Ud. recordó

Nosotros recordamos

Vosotros recordasteis

Ellos/Ellas/Uds. recordaron

RECORDAR

THE PRESENT TENSE	THE PRETERITE TENSE
Yo _____ que vivíamos en el tercer piso.	Ellos no _____ que hoy es el cumpleaños de Joaquín.
Nosotros _____ el dinero cada mañana.	Tú _____ que tenemos un examen hoy.
Ellos no _____ llamar a casa cuando se van.	¿Por que no _____ ellos traer el bolso?
¿Por qué no _____ él la chaqueta cuando hace frío?	Nosotros _____ llamar a mamá anoche.
Tú _____ que vamos al hospital hoy.	Yo no _____ lavar mis pantalones.

ROBAR
to steal

rroh-bahr

KEYWORD:
robber...*steals*
robar

The **rob**ber *steals* the wheels

PRESENT TENSE
Yo robo
Tú robas
Él/Ella/Ud. roba
Nosotros robamos
Vosotros robáis
Ellos/Ellas/Uds. roban

PRETERITE TENSE
Yo robé
Tú robaste
Él/Ella/Ud. robó
Nosotros robamos
Vosotros robasteis
Ellos/Ellas/Uds. robaron

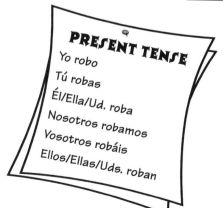

ROBAR

THE PRESENT TENSE	THE PRETERITE TENSE
Nosotros _____ el dinero del banco.	Él no _____ los papeles del profesor.
Yo no _____ cosas que no son mías.	Tú no _____ el dinero.
Ella _____ lo que quiere.	Yo no _____ nunca.
¿Cuándo _____ tú las galletas de tu hermano?	¿ _____ ellas los pasaportes?
Ellos _____ las chaquetas de sus compañeros.	Mariano no _____ los guantes de Juan.

SABER

to know

sah-behr

KEYWORD:
saber..._know_
saber

What do you **_know_** about **saber** tooth tigers?

PRESENT TENSE

Yo sé

Tú sabes

Él/Ella/Ud. sabe

Nosotros sabemos

Vosotros sabéis

Ellos/Ellas/Uds. saben

PRETERITE TENSE

Yo supe

Tú supiste

Él/Ella/Ud. supo

Nosotros supimos

Vosotros supisteis

Ellos/Ellas/Uds. supieron

SABER

THE PRESENT TENSE	THE PRETERITE TENSE
Yo _____ que hora es.	Ella _____ las noticias de su hermano.
Ellos no _____ que hoy es martes.	Yo no _____ nada hasta que hablé con mi primo.
Nosotros _____ que la calle está por aquí.	Ellos lo _____ cuando vieron la maleta.
¿_____ tú dónde vive Nicole?	¿Cuándo _____ tú que Margarita no se iba a casar?
Ella _____ que el avión sale en diez minutos.	Nosotros _____ que el viaje fue cancelado.

SACAR
to take out

sah-kahr

KEYWORD:
sack...**_takes out_**
sacar

Mack **_takes_** the rabbit **_out_** of a **sac**k

PRESENT TENSE

Yo saco

Tú sacas

Él/Ella/Ud. saca

Nosotros sacamos

Vosotros sacáis

Ellos/Ellas/Uds. sacan

PRETERITE TENSE

Yo saqué

Tú sacaste

Él/Ella/Ud. sacó

Nosotros sacamos

Vosotros sacasteis

Ellos/Ellas/Uds. sacaron

SACAR

THE PRESENT TENSE	THE PRETERITE TENSE
Yo _____ buenas notas en los examenes.	Él no _____ su mejor traje para la fiesta.
Tú no _____ la basura por la mañana.	Tú _____ malas notas en el colegio.
¿Cuándo _____ Miguel la comida?	Nosotros _____ la cama del armario.
Nosotros no _____ el perro por la noche.	Yo _____ un lápiz para el examen.
Ella _____ el mejor vino cuando vamos a su casa.	Uds. no _____ nada especial para la visita.

SALIR
to leave

sah-leer

KEYWORD:
saloon...*__leaves__*
salir

Boone *__leaves__* the **sal**oon

PRESENT TENSE

Yo salgo

Tú sales

Él/Ella/Ud. sale

Nosotros salimos

Vosotros salís

Ellos/Ellas/Uds. salen

PRETERITE TENSE

Yo salí

Tú saliste

Él/Ella/Ud. salió

Nosotros salimos

Vosotros salisteis

Ellos/Ellas/Uds. salieron

SALIR

THE PRESENT TENSE	THE PRETERITE TENSE
Ellos _____ a las ocho.	Ella _____ con Miguel anoche.
Nosotros no _____ con los vecinos.	Yo no _____ porque estaba cansado.
Yo _____ cada viernes.	¿Por qué no _____ ellos con sus amigos?
¿ _____ tú con tus primos este fin de semana?	Nosotros _____ pero volvimos a casa en seguida.
Ud. _____ para comprar leche.	Ana y Pepe _____ a ver una película.

SALUDAR
to greet

sah-loo-dahr

KEYWORD:
salute...**_greet_**
saludar

The recruits **_greet_** me with a **salu**te

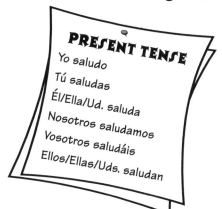

PRESENT TENSE

Yo saludo

Tú saludas

Él/Ella/Ud. saluda

Nosotros saludamos

Vosotros saludáis

Ellos/Ellas/Uds. saludan

PRETERITE TENSE

Yo saludé

Tú saludaste

Él/Ella/Ud. saludó

Nosotros saludamos

Vosotros saludasteis

Ellos/Ellas/Uds. saludaron

SALUDAR

THE PRESENT TENSE	THE PRETERITE TENSE
Yo _____ al profesor todos los días.	¿ _____ tú cuando llegaste?
Ellos no _____ porque no conocen al portero.	Ella _____ cuando me vio.
Tú _____ cada vez que entras.	Nosotros no _____ al presidente del club.
¿Por qué no _____ ellos cuando nos ven?	¿Por qué no _____ Mario cuando llamó?
Nosotros _____ de costumbre.	Yo _____ porque soy una persona amable.

SUBIR
to go up

soo-beer

KEYWORD:
sub...*goes up*
subir

The **sub *goes up*** in the tub

PRESENT TENSE
Yo subo
Tú subes
Él/Ella/Ud. sube
Nosotros subimos
Vosotros subís
Ellos/Ellas/Uds. suben

PRETERITE TENSE
Yo subí
Tú subiste
Él/Ella/Ud. subió
Nosotros subimos
Vosotros subisteis
Ellos/Ellas/Uds. subieron

SUBIR

Nosotros _____ la montaña.

Tú _____ la escalera.

Ellos no _____ porque les da miedo.

¿Cuándo _____ él al ático?

Yo _____ todos los días a las nueve.

Ellas no _____ la roca.

Yo _____ a hablar con Miguel.

Nosotros _____ al techo para sacar el disco.

¿ _____ tú el dinero a Pepe?

Marcos _____ la cuesta andando.

SUSPENDER

to fail

KEYWORD:
suspended...*failing*
suspender

Les is **suspend**ed for *failing* a test

PRESENT TENSE

Yo suspendo

Tú suspendes

Él/Ella/Ud. suspende

Nosotros suspendemos

Vosotros suspendéis

Ellos/Ellas/Uds. suspenden

PRETERITE TENSE

Yo suspendí

Tú suspendiste

Él/Ella/Ud. suspendió

Nosotros suspendimos

Vosotros suspendisteis

Ellos/Ellas/Uds. suspendieron

SUSPENDER

THE PRESENT TENSE	THE PRETERITE TENSE
Ellos _____ todos los exámenes.	¿ _____ tú el examen final?
Nosotros _____ porque no estudiamos.	Ella _____ porque no leyó la historia.
Yo no _____ porque soy buen estudiante.	Nosotros no _____ porque somos inteligentes.
¿ _____ él la clase de español?	Yo _____ el proyecto porque mi compañero no hizo nada.
Tú _____ las clases difíciles.	Mis hermanos nunca _____ un examen de historia.

TENER
to have

teh-nehr

KEYWORD:
ten...**_has_**
tener

Sam Smothers **_has_** **ten** brothers

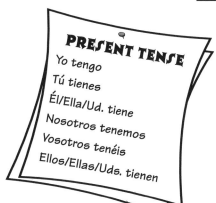

PRESENT TENSE
Yo tengo
Tú tienes
Él/Ella/Ud. tiene
Nosotros tenemos
Vosotros tenéis
Ellos/Ellas/Uds. tienen

PRETERITE TENSE
Yo tuve
Tú tuviste
Él/Ella/Ud. tuvo
Nosotros tuvimos
Vosotros tuvisteis
Ellos/Ellas/Uds. tuvieron

TENER

THE PRESENT TENSE	THE PRETERITE TENSE
Yo _____ dos hermanos.	Ella _____ noticias de Angel ayer.
Ellos no _____ mucho dinero.	Ellos _____ una fiesta el domingo pasado.
Tú no _____ un coche para llegar.	Nosotros _____ el trofeo por un año.
¿ _____ Uds. un garaje?	¿ _____ tú un accidente ayer?
Nosotros _____ muchos amigos.	Mario _____ una llamada rara anoche.

TERMINAR

tehr-mee-nahr

to end

KEYWORD:
terminator...**_ends_**
terminar

"No way the **termina**tor **_ends_** today!"

PRESENT TENSE
Yo termino
Tú terminas
Él/Ella/Ud. termina
Nosotros terminamos
Vosotros termináis
Ellos/Ellas/Uds. terminan

PRETERITE TENSE
Yo terminé
Tú terminaste
Él/Ella/Ud. terminó
Nosotros terminamos
Vosotros terminasteis
Ellos/Ellas/Uds. terminaron

TERMINAR

THE PRESENT TENSE	THE PRETERITE TENSE
Él _____ el examen a tiempo.	Nosotros _____ las invitaciones a las doce.
Ellos no _____ el proyecto.	Yo _____ la película antes de ir a trabajar.
Yo _____ cada libro que empiezo.	Tú no _____ el recorrido.
¿ _____ tú de estudiar tarde?	¿ _____ ellos el calendario para el año que viene?
Nosotros _____ todos los días a las ocho.	Por fin Margarita _____ de explicar el problema.

TIRAR
to throw

KEYWORD:
tires…***throw***
tirar

"Let's ***throw*** **tir**es into the fire!"

PRESENT TENSE
Yo tiro
Tú tiras
Él/Ella/Ud. tira
Nosotros tiramos
Vosotros tiráis
Ellos/Ellas/Uds. tiran

PRETERITE TENSE
Yo tiré
Tú tiraste
Él/Ella/Ud. tiró
Nosotros tiramos
Vosotros tirasteis
Ellos/Ellas/Uds. tiraron

TIRAR

THE PRESENT TENSE	THE PRETERITE TENSE
Él _____ la basura cada mañana.	Yo no _____ la revista por la ventana.
Nosotros _____ la pelota.	Ellas _____ los globos a los niños.
Tú no _____ papeles en el suelo.	¿Por qué _____ tú las pesas al suelo?
Uds. _____ los libros a la mesa.	Juan _____ el dinero a los niños.
¿ _____ Ud. los folletos al aire?	Nosotros _____ el vestido a la basura.

TOCAR
to play (an instrument)

toh-kahr

KEYWORD:
toes...**_plays_**
tocar

Joe **_plays_** piano with his **to**es

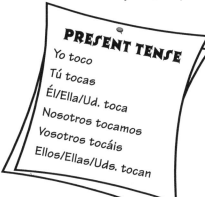

PRESENT TENSE
Yo toco
Tú tocas
Él/Ella/Ud. toca
Nosotros tocamos
Vosotros tocáis
Ellos/Ellas/Uds. tocan

PRETERITE TENSE
Yo toqué
Tú tocaste
Él/Ella/Ud. tocó
Nosotros tocamos
Vosotros tocasteis
Ellos/Ellas/Uds. tocaron

TOCAR

THE PREJENT TENJE	THE PRETERITE TENJE
Ella _____ el piano muy bien.	Tú _____ en la orquesta.
Yo no _____ ningún instrumento.	¿ _____ ellos anoche en el club?
Nosotros _____ con la banda cada noche.	Yo no _____ porque estaba enfermo.
¿Dónde _____ tú la bateria?	Nosotros _____ porque nos pagaron bien.
Ud. _____ como un profesional.	Mi hermano _____ la guitarra en la fiesta.

TOMAR
to take

toh-mahr

KEYWORD:
Tom..._takes_
Tomar

Tom _takes_ a test with his mom

EXAM NAME: Tom

PRESENT TENSE

Yo tomo

Tú tomas

Él/Ella/Ud. toma

Nosotros tomamos

Vosotros tomáis

Ellos/Ellas/Uds. toman

PRETERITE TENSE

Yo tomé

Tú tomaste

Él/Ella/Ud. tomó

Nosotros tomamos

Vosotros tomasteis

Ellos/Ellas/Uds. tomaron

TOMAR

THE PRESENT TENSE	THE PRETERITE TENSE
Yo no _____ el examen porque no quiero.	Ud. no _____ el quizcito ayer.
Nosotros no _____ los apuntes.	Yo _____ mi examen de historia esta mañana.
Ellos _____ el curso porque es obligatorio.	Tú _____ muchas notas en clase.
¿ _____ ella el avión a las cinco?	¿Por qué _____ ellos el helado?
Tú _____ mucho tiempo para terminar.	Nosotros _____ las medidas.

TRABAJAR
to work

trah-bah-**hahr**

KEYWORD:
Traba…*works*
Trabajar

Traba ***works*** at his jobba

PRESENT TENSE

Yo trabajo
Tú trabajas
Él/Ella/Ud. trabaja
Nosotros trabajamos
Vosotros trabajáis
Ellos/Ellas/Uds. trabajan

PRETERITE TENSE

Yo trabajé
Tú trabajaste
Él/Ella/Ud. trabajó
Nosotros trabajamos
Vosotros trabajasteis
Ellos/Ellas/Uds. trabajaron

TRABAJAR

THE PRESENT TENSE	THE PRETERITE TENSE
Juan _____ mucho.	Mario _____ anoche.
Nosotros _____ en la tienda.	Los padres _____ hasta muy tarde.
Ud. no _____ los lunes.	Yo _____ poco.
¿ _____ tú a las dos?	¿ _____ ellas en el concierto?
Yo _____ con tu padre.	Tú no _____ en el supermercado.

TRAER
to bring

trah-yehr

KEYWORD:
tra y...**brings**
traer

Ray **brings** a dessert **tra**y

PRESENT TENSE
Yo traigo
Tú traes
Él/Ella/Ud. trae
Nosotros traemos
Vosotros traéis
Ellos/Ellas/Uds. traen

PRETERITE TENSE
Yo traje
Tú trajiste
Él/Ella/Ud. trajo
Nosotros trajimos
Vosotros trajisteis
Ellos/Ellas/Uds. trajeron

TRAER

THE PRESENT TENSE	THE PRETERITE TENSE
Ellas _____ los aperitivos a la fiesta.	Uds. _____ la música.
Yo no _____ nada.	¿Cuándo _____ tú la nevera?
Nosotros _____ las llaves a Juan.	Nosotros no _____ la tarea.
¿ _____ tú el coche nuevo?	Yo _____ el dinero.
Él no _____ a su bebé.	Ud. no _____ la información.

VENDER
to sell

behn-dehr

KEYWORD:
vendor...**sells**
vender

The **vend**or **sells** to his customer

PRESENT TENSE
Yo vendo
Tú vendes
Él/Ella/Ud. vende
Nosotros vendemos
Vosotros vendéis
Ellos/Ellas/Uds. venden

PRETERITE TENSE
Yo vendí
Tú vendiste
Él/Ella/Ud. vendió
Nosotros vendimos
Vosotros vendisteis
Ellos/Ellas/Uds. vendieron

VENDER

THE PRESENT TENSE	THE PRETERITE TENSE
Yo _____ mi coche.	Ella _____ su anillo ayer.
Tú no _____ el reloj.	Tú no _____ las fotos de la boda.
Nosotros _____ los diamantes.	Yo _____ un pastel a mi hermano.
¿ _____ ellos su piano?	Nosotros _____ los ensayos que escribimos.
Uds. _____ el sofá porque es viejo.	¿ _____ Pedro la casa?

VENIR
to come

beh-**neer**

KEYWORD:
ven om…***come***
venir

Come ven om…***come*** on **ven** om…good boy!

PRESENT TENSE

Yo vengo

Tú vienes

Él/Ella/Ud. viene

Nosotros venimos

Vosotros venís

Ellos/Ellas/Uds. vienen

PRETERITE TENSE

Yo vine

Tú viniste

Él/Ella/Ud. vino

Nosotros vinimos

Vosotros vinisteis

Ellos/Ellas/Uds. vinieron

VENIR

THE PRESENT TENSE	THE PRETERITE TENSE
Ella _____ a las tres.	Ellos no _____ hasta muy tarde.
Nosotros _____ cuando la fiesta empieza.	Tú _____ cuando la música empezó.
Yo no _____ si no está Gloria.	Nosotros _____ con el novio.
Tú _____ si tienen dulces.	¿ _____ ella en su coche nuevo?
¿ _____ Uds. con las gambas?	Mario _____ porque él quería ver a Ana.

VER
to see

behr

KEYWORD:
Verb...**see**
ver

* BASIC ENGLISH GRAMMAR
Which word is the verb?

THE DOG SEES THE CAT IN THE TREE.

Hey, over here!

Hey Bozo,
what about this one?

Herb finally **see** the **ver**b

PRESENT TENSE
Yo veo
Tú ves
Él/Ella/Ud. ve
Nosotros vemos
Vosotros veis
Ellos/Ellas/Uds. ven

PRETERITE TENSE
Yo vi
Tú viste
Él/Ella/Ud. vio
Nosotros vimos
Vosotros visteis
Ellos/Ellas/Uds. vieron

VER

THE PRESENT TENSE	THE PRETERITE TENSE
Ellas _____ el coche en la calle.	Él _____ el accidente.
Ud. no _____ la pizarra desde su silla.	Yo _____ a José en la fiesta.
Nosotros _____ que hay un problema	Uds. no _____ la casa.
Yo no _____ nada.	¿ _____ ella la ceremonia?
¿ _____ tú que ella es rubia?	Nosotros _____ el avión.

VIAJAR
to travel

KEYWORD:
via...*travel*
viajar

On Mars, they **travel** via jars

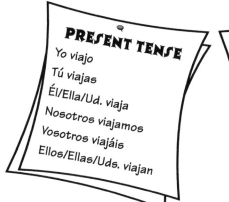

PRESENT TENSE
Yo viajo
Tú viajas
Él/Ella/Ud. viaja
Nosotros viajamos
Vosotros viajáis
Ellos/Ellas/Uds. viajan

PRETERITE TENSE
Yo viajé
Tú viajaste
Él/Ella/Ud. viajó
Nosotros viajamos
Vosotros viajasteis
Ellos/Ellas/Uds. viajaron

VIAJAR

THE PRESENT TENSE	THE PRETERITE TENSE
Ellas _____ a Japón.	Él no _____ porque le daba miedo.
Yo no _____ por tren.	
	Ellos _____ a la costa.
Tú _____ por la ciudad.	
	Nosotros _____ en grupos de cinco.
Nosotros _____ por la mañana.	
	¿ _____ tú el año pasado?
¿ _____ Uds. con los primos?	Yo _____ por todo el país.

VIVIR
to live

bee-beer

KEYWORD:
Viv…**lives**
Vivir

Viv **lives** with her relatives

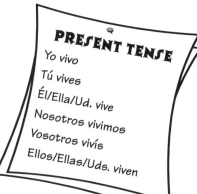

PRESENT TENSE
Yo vivo
Tú vives
Él/Ella/Ud. vive
Nosotros vivimos
Vosotros vivís
Ellos/Ellas/Uds. viven

PRETERITE TENSE
Yo viví
Tú viviste
Él/Ella/Ud. vivió
Nosotros vivimos
Vosotros vivisteis
Ellos/Ellas/Uds. vivieron

VIVIR

THE PRESENT TENSE	THE PRETERITE TENSE
Yo no _____ en California.	Tú no _____ en un barco.
Ellas _____ cerca de la playa.	Nosotros _____ en una isla por un año.
Tú _____ con tus padres.	Yo no _____ con mis primas el año pasado.
¿ _____ ellos en una casa?	¿ _____ Juan con Maria antes?
Ud. _____ en una mansión.	Los niños _____ con sus abuelos.

VOLAR
to fly

boh-lahr

KEYWORD:
volleyball…_**flies**_
volar

The **vol**leyball _**flies**_ to the sky

PRESENT TENSE
Yo vuelo

Tú vuelas

Él/Ella/Ud. vuela

Nosotros volamos

Vosotros voláis

Ellos/Ellas/Uds. vuelan

PRETERITE TENSE
Yo volé

Tú volaste

Él/Ella/Ud. voló

Nosotros volamos

Vosotros volasteis

Ellos/Ellas/Uds. volaron

VOLAR

THE PRESENT TENSE	THE PRETERITE TENSE
Yo no _____ con esa compañia.	El año pasado tú _____ en un avión pequeño.
Tú _____ en globo.	Ella _____ a España ayer.
Uds. _____ por la noche.	Nosotros _____ con las compañías más fuertes.
¿ _____ ellos en un 747?	¿ _____ Mario anoche?
Nosotros _____ juntos a todas partes.	Yo no _____ porque se canceló el vuelo.

VOLVER
to return

bohl-behr

KEYWORD:
volvo...**_returns_**
volver

Manolo **_returns_** in a **volv**o

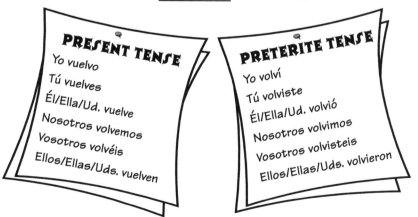

PRESENT TENSE
Yo vuelvo
Tú vuelves
Él/Ella/Ud. vuelve
Nosotros volvemos
Vosotros volvéis
Ellos/Ellas/Uds. vuelven

PRETERITE TENSE
Yo volví
Tú volviste
Él/Ella/Ud. volvió
Nosotros volvimos
Vosotros volvisteis
Ellos/Ellas/Uds. volvieron

VOLVER

THE PRESENT TENSE	THE PRETERITE TENSE
Ud. _____ a la misma hora.	Ellos no _____ a tiempo.
Nosotros _____ cada día a las cinco.	Tú _____ para estar con la familia.
Ellos _____ para tomar el examen.	¿ _____ Ud. esta tarde?
¿ _____ él para celebrar el cumpleaños?	Nosotros _____ a nuestra casa.
Tú no _____ porque no quieres.	Yo no _____ porque no tenía dinero.

THE PRESENT TENSE

Subject Pronouns

When any verb is conjugated in Spanish, these are the subject pronouns used.

Yo – I
Tú – You (informal)
Él – He
Ella – She
Usted (Ud.) – You (formal)

Nosotros/Nosotras – We
Vosotros/Vosotras – You (informal, pl.)
Ellos – They (a group with at least one male)
Ellas – They (a group with all females)
Ustedes (Uds.) – You (formal/informal, pl.)

VERBS

Verbs end in either **-ar, -er, -ir.**

Examples:

-ar	**-er**	**-ir**
hablar	leer	abrir
ayudar	comer	recibir

Regular Verbs

All verbs cut off the **-ar, -er, -ir** endings and what is left is called the stem.

Example: Hablar - habl
            Comer - com
            Vivir -   viv

The **–ar, -er, -ir** personal endings that follow are added to the stem:

-ar verbs

Yo -	**o**	Nosotros -	**amos**	
Tú -	**as**	Vosotros -	**áis**	
Él -	**a**	Ellos -	**an**	
Ella -	**a**	Ellas -	**an**	
Ud. -	**a**	Uds. -	**an**	

Example:

Hablar - to speak

Yo	habl**o**	I speak	Nosotros	habl**amos**	We speak
Tú	habl**as**	You speak	Vosotros	habl**áis**	You speak
Él	habl**a**	He speaks	Ellos	habl**an**	They speak
Ella	habl**a**	She speaks	Ellas	habl**an**	They speak
Ud.	habl**a**	You speak	Uds.	habl**an**	You speak

. 201 .

-er verbs

Yo -	**o**	Nosotros -	**emos**
Tú -	**es**	Vosotros -	**éis**
Él -	**e**	Ellos -	**en**
Ella -	**e**	Ellas -	**en**
Ud. -	**e**	Uds. -	**en**

<u>Example:</u>

Comer - to eat

Yo	com**o**	I eat	Nosotros	com**emos**	We eat
Tú	com**es**	You eat	Vosotros	com**éis**	You eat
Él	com**e**	He eats	Ellos	com**en**	They (m) eat
Ella	com**e**	She eats	Ellas	com**en**	They (f) eat
Ud.	com**e**	You eat	Uds.	com**en**	You eat

-ir verbs

Yo -	**o**	Nosotros -	**imos**
Tú -	**es**	Vosotros -	**ís**
Él -	**e**	Ellos -	**en**
Ella -	**e**	Ellas -	**en**
Ud. -	**e**	Uds. -	**en**

<u>Example :</u>

Vivir - to live

Yo	viv**o**	I live	Nosotros	viv**imos**	We live
Tú	viv**es**	You live	Vosotros	viv**ís**	You live
Él	viv**e**	He lives	Ellos	viv**en**	They (m) live
Ella	viv**e**	She lives	Ellas	viv**en**	They (f) live
Ud.	viv**e**	You live	Uds.	viv**en**	You live

Reflexive Verbs

These verbs are recognized by the **-se** at the end. If you take off the **-se** you will find an **-ar, -er, -ir** verb that needs to be conjugated.
All reflexive verbs need a reflexive pronoun.

1. These are the reflexive pronouns with their respective subject pronouns. They are included in the conjugation.

Yo -	**me**	Nosotros -	**nos**
Tú -	**te**	Vosotros -	**os**
Él -	**se**	Ellos -	**se**
Ella -	**se**	Ellas -	**se**
Ud. -	**se**	Uds. -	**se**

2. Look at the verb that's left after taking off the **-se**.
Example:

llamarse - llamar
Llamar is a regular verb so its conjugation is the same as other regular **-ar** verbs. You combine the reflexive pronouns with the verb form:

Yo	**me** llamo	Nosotros	**nos** llamamos
Tú	**te** llamas	Vosotros	**os** llamáis
Él	**se** llama	Ellos	**se** llaman
Ella	**se** llama	Ellas	**se** llaman
Ud.	**se** llama	Uds.	**se** llaman

The Irregular Verbs
These verbs are called irregular because they have some change that prevents them from following the rules that the regular verbs follow.

Group 1 - Stem-changing verbs.

E-IE - Verbs that change the **E** in their stem to **IE** in all forms except nosotros/vosotros.

Querer - to want
Quer - the stem

Yo	quiero	Nosotros	queremos
Tú	quieres	Vosotros	queréis
Él	quiere	Ellos	quieren
Ella	quiere	Ellas	quieren
Ud.	quiere	Uds.	quieren

Other verbs that have the same changes:
cerrar   perder   pensar
despertarse   atender   comenzar

O-UE - Verbs that change the **O** in their stem to **UE** in all forms except nosotros/vosotros.

Volver - to return
Volv- the stem

Yo	vuelvo	Nosotros	volvemos
Tú	vuelves	Vosotros	volvéis
Él	vuelve	Ellos	vuelven
Ella	vuelve	Ellas	vuelven
Ud.	vuelve	Uds.	vuelven

Other verbs that have the same changes:
almorzar   dormir   jugar (u-ue)   poder
encontrar   recordar   acostarse

E-I - Verbs that change the **E** in their stem to **I** in all forms except nosotros/vosotros.

Pedir - to ask for
Ped - the stem

Yo	pido	Nosotros	pedimos
Tú	pides	Vosotros	pedís
Él	pide	Ellos	piden
Ella	pide	Ellas	piden
Ud.	pide	Uds.	piden

Other verbs that have the same changes:
servir   repetir   vestirse

Group 2 - Verbs that have **"GO"** in the yo form but then follow the rules for conjugating regular verbs.

Salir - to leave
Sal - the stem

Yo	salgo	Nosotros	salimos
Tú	sales	Vosotros	salís
Él	sale	Ellos	salen
Ella	sale	Ellas	salen
Ud.	sale	Uds.	salen

Other verbs that have the same change:
Caer -   caigo
Hacer - hago
Poner - pongo
Traer - traigo

Group 3 - Verbs that have **"GO"** in the yo form and then have other changes:
Decir - digo, dices, dice, dice, decimos, decís, dicen
Venir - vengo, vienes, viene, venimos, venís, vienen
Oír - oigo, oyes, oye, oímos, oís, oyen
Tener - tengo, tienes, tiene, tenemos, tenéis, tienen

Group 4 - Verbs that have changes in the **"YO"** form but are regular in the rest of the conjugation:
Ver - veo, ves, ve, vemos, veis, ven
Dar - doy, das, da, damos, dais, dan
Ir - voy, vas, va, vamos, vais, van (v + -ar endings)
Saber - sé, sabes, sabe, sabemos, sabéis, saben
Conocer - conozco, conoces, conoce, conocemos, conocéis, conocen
Conducir -conduzco, conduces, conduce, conducimos, conducís, conducen

Group 5 - Verbs that end in **-UIR** (doesn't include -GUIR verbs) add a **"Y"** to the stem before conjugating in all forms except nosotros/vosotros.

Construir - to build
Constru - the stem

Yo	construyo	Nosotros	construímos
Tú	construyes	Vosotros	construís
Él	construye	Ellos	construyen
Ella	construye	Ellas	construyen
Ud.	construye	Uds.	construyen

Other verbs that have the same changes:
Destruir   concluir

THE PRETERITE
(THE PAST TENSE)

Verbs that are conjugated to convey actions in the past are said to be conjugated in the preterite tense. Like the present tense, there are regular verbs which follow a pattern and irregulars which, for the most part, do not.

Regular Verbs

The endings for the **-ar, -er, -ir** verbs are as follows:

-ar verbs

Yo -	**é**	Nosotros -	**amos**
Tú -	**aste**	Vosotros -	**asteis**
Él -	**ó**	Ellos -	**aron**
Ella -	**ó**	Ellas -	**aron**
Ud. -	**ó**	Uds.-	**aron**

Hablar - to speak

Yo	habl**é**	I spoke	Nosotros	habl**amos**	We spoke
Tú	habl**aste**	You spoke	Vosotros	habl**asteis**	You spoke
Él	habl**ó**	He spoke	Ellos	habl**aron**	They spoke
Ella	habl**ó**	She spoke	Ellas	habl**aron**	They spoke
Ud.	habl**ó**	You spoke	Uds.	habl**aron**	You spoke

-er / - ir verbs

Yo -	**í**	Nosotros -	**imos**
Tú -	**iste**	Vosotros -	**isteis**
Él -	**ió**	Ellos -	**ieron**
Ella -	**ió**	Ellas -	**ieron**
Ud. -	**ió**	Uds. -	**ieron**

Comer - to eat

Yo	com**í**	I ate	Nosotros	com**imos**	We ate
Tú	com**iste**	You ate	Vosotros	com**isteis**	You ate
Él	com**ió**	He ate	Ellos	com**ieron**	They (m) ate
Ella	com**ió**	She ate	Ellas	com**ieron**	They (f) ate
Ud.	com**ió**	You ate	Uds.	com**ieron**	You ate

Vivir - to live

Yo	viv**í**	I lived	Nosotros	viv**imos**	We lived
Tú	viv**iste**	You lived	Vosotros	viv**isteis**	You lived
Él	viv**ió**	He lived	Ellos	viv**ieron**	They (m) lived
Ella	viv**ió**	She lived	Ellas	viv**ieron**	They (f) lived
Ud.	viv**ió**	You lived	Uds.	viv**ieron**	You lived

The Irregular Verbs

Keeping in mind that there are patterns in small groups in the irregular category, we will start with group number 1

Group 1 - Verbs that end in -car, -gar, -zar.

-car	-gar	-zar
sacar	llegar	cruzar
practicar	pagar	almorzar

These verbs have one change in the **"YO"** form. However, the rest of the conjugation is normal.

The changes are as follows:

-CAR

Sacar becomes "Yo sa**qué**." The **"c"** changes to **"qu"**.

Yo	sa**qué**	Nosotros	sac**amos**
Tú	sac**aste**	Vosotros	sac**asteis**
Él	sac**ó**	Ellos	sac**aron**
Ella	sac**ó**	Ellas	sac**aron**
Ud.	sac**ó**	Uds.	sac**aron**

-GAR

Llegar becomes "Yo lle**gué**." The **"g"** changes to **"gu"**.

Yo	lle**gué**	Nosotros	lleg**amos**
Tú	lleg**aste**	Vosotros	lleg**asteis**
Él	lleg**ó**	Ellos	lleg**aron**
Ella	lleg**ó**	Ellas	lleg**aron**
Ud.	lleg**ó**	Uds.	lleg**aron**

-ZAR

Alcanzar becomes "Yo alcan**cé**." The **"z"** changes to **"c"**.

Yo	alcan**cé**	Nosotros	alcanz**amos**
Tú	alcanz**aste**	Vosotros	alcanz**asteis**
Él	alcanz**ó**	Ellos	alcanz**aron**
Ella	alcanz**ó**	Ellas	alcanz**aron**
Ud.	alcanz**ó**	Uds.	alcanz**aron**

Group 2 - This group is made up of verbs that have different stems but do share common endings. There are no accents!

Tener   tuv
Estar   estuv
Venir   vin   **Endings**
Poner   pus   Yo - **e**   Nosotros - **imos**
Poder   pud   Tú - **iste**   Vosotros - **isteis**
Querer   quis   Él - **o**   Ellos -   **ieron**
Saber   sup   Ella - **o**   Ellas -   **ieron**
Hacer   hic*   Ud. - **o**   Uds. -   **ieron**
Decir   dij**
Conducir   conduj**
Traer   traj**

*This verb shares all the forms except él/ella/Ud.
Hacer   Él hizo

**These verbs share all forms except ellos/ellas/Uds.
Decir   Ellos dijeron
Conducir   Ellas condujeron
Traer   Uds. trajeron

Group 3 - Other verbs that have something in common:

Dar

Di	Dimos
Diste	Disteis
Dio	Dieron

Ver

Vi	Vimos
Viste	Visteis
Vio	Vieron

- No accents
- Only difference between the two is the first letter.

Ser / Ir

Fui	Fuimos
Fuiste	Fuisteis
Fue	Fueron

- No accents
- Same exact conjugation for both verbs!

Group 4 - Verbs that have changes only in the él/ella/Ud, ellos/ellas/Uds:

dormir (u)

dormí	dormimos
dormiste	dormisteis
dUrmió	**dUrmieron**

Pedir (i)

pedí	pedimos
pediste	pedisteis
pIdió	**pIdieron**

Other verbs: repetir (i), servir (i), vestirse (i)

Group 5 - Verbs that change the I to a Y in the él/ella/Ud. and ellos/ellas/Uds. forms. Also, along with the accents found on yo and él/ella/ud, they add accents to the Tú and the Nosotros/Vosotros forms as well.

Creer

creí	creímos
creíste	creísteis
creyó	creyeron

Other verbs: leer, oír, caerse.

QUICK REFERENCE

Abrir	To open
Alcanzar	To reach
Alquilar	To rent
Almorzar	To eat lunch
Aprender	To learn
Arreglar	To fix
Asistir	To attend
Atender	To attend to
Ayudar	To help
Bailar	To dance
Beber	To drink
Buscar	To look for
Caerse	To fall down
Cambiar	To change
Caminar	To walk
Cantar	To sing
Cenar	To eat dinner
Cerrar	To close
Cocinar	To cook
Comenzar	To begin
Comer	To eat
Comprar	To buy
Comprender	To understand
Conducir	To drive
Conocer	To know (people, places, things)

Construir	To build
Contestar	To answer
Correr	To run
Cortar	To cut
Creer	To believe
Cruzar	To cross
Cubrir	To cover
Dar	To give
Decir	To say, tell
Dejar	To leave behind
Descansar	To rest
Despertarse	To wake up
Dormir	To sleep
Durar	To last
Encontrar	To find
Enfermarse	To get sick
Escribir	To write
Escuchar	To listen to
Esperar	To wait for
Estudiar	To study
Evitar	To avoid
Fumar	To smoke
Ganar	To win
Gastar	To spend
Gritar	To shout
Hablar	To speak
Hacer	To do, make
Ir	To go

Jugar	To play
Levantarse	To get up
Lavarse	To wash yourself
Leer	To read
Limpiar	To clean
Llamar	To call
Llegar	To arrive
Llevar	To wear
Mandar	To send
Meter	To put in
Mirar	To look at
Nadar	To swim
Odiar	To hate
Oír	To hear
Parar	To stop
Pedir	To ask for
Pegar	To hit
Pensar	To think
Perder	To lose
Poner	To put
Preguntar	To ask
Prometer	To promise
Querer	To want
Recibir	To receive
Recordar	To remember
Robar	To rob
Saber	To know (facts)
Sacar	To take out

Salir	To leave
Saludar	To greet
Subir	To go up
Suspender	To fail
Tener	To have
Terminar	To end
Tirar	To throw
Tocar	To play (an instrument)
Tomar	To take
Trabajar	To work
Traer	To bring
Vender	To sell
Venir	To come
Ver	To see
Viajar	To travel
Volar	To fly
Volver	To return
Vivir	To live

ANSWER KEY

PRESENT	PRETERITE	PRESENT	PRETERITE
Abrir	**p. 2**	**Alcanzar**	**p. 4**
abro	abrió	alcanza	alcanzó
abre	abrieron	alcanzamos	alcanzaron
abrimos	abriste	alcanza	alcanzaste
abren	abrió	alcanzas	alcanzaron
abres	abrí	alcanzo	alcancé
Almorzar	**p. 6**	**Alquilar**	**p. 8**
almuerzo	almorzó	alquila	alquiló
almorzamos	almorzaste	alquilan	alquilamos
almuerza	almorcé	alquilas	alquiló
almuerzan	almorzaron	alquilamos	alquilé
almuerzas	almorzó	alquilo	alquilaron
Aprender	**p. 10**	**Arreglar**	**p. 12**
aprendo	aprendieron	arregla	arreglamos
aprenden	aprendí	arreglamos	arregló
aprendemos	aprendió	arreglan	arreglaste
aprendes	aprendió	arregla	arreglaron
aprende	aprendiste	arreglas	arreglé
Asistir	**p. 14**	**Atender**	**p. 16**
asiste	asistieron	atiende	atendieron
asisto	asististe	atienden	atendí
asisten	asistieron	atiendes	atendiste
asistes	asistió	atienden	atendió
asistimos	asistí	atiendo	atendimos
Ayudar	**p. 18**	**Bailar**	**p. 20**
ayudas	ayudó	baila	bailaron
ayuda	ayudamos	bailamos	bailé
ayudan	ayudaron	bailo	bailó
ayudamos	ayudé	bailas	bailamos
ayudo	ayudaste	baila	bailaron

ANSWER KEY

PRESENT	PRETERITE	PRESENT	PRETERITE
Beber	p. 22	Buscar	p. 24
bebo	bebió	buscas	busqué
beben	bebimos	busco	buscó
bebes	bebieron	buscan	buscaste
bebemos	bebiste	buscamos	buscó
bebe	bebí	busca	buscaron
Caerse	p. 26	Cambiar	p. 28
me caigo	me caí	cambian	cambié
se cae	nos caímos	cambiamos	cambiaron
nos caemos	se cayeron	cambio	cambiaste
se caen	se cayó	cambia	cambió
te caes	te caíste	cambias	cambiaron
Caminar	p. 30	Cantar	p. 32
caminamos	caminé	canta	cantaron
caminan	caminó	cantan	cantó
camina	caminaron	canto	cantó
caminas	caminaste	cantas	cantamos
caminan	caminamos	cantamos	canté
Cenar	p. 34	Cerrar	p. 36
ceno	cenaste	cierra	cerré
cenan	cenó	cierras	cerraron
cenan	cenaron	cierro	cerramos
cena	cené	cierra	cerró
cenamos	cenaron	cerramos	cerraste
Cocinar	p. 38	Comenzar	p. 40
cocina	cocinó	comienza	comenzó
cocinamos	cocinaron	comenzamos	comenzaron
cocina	cocinó	comienzas	comenzaste
cocinas	cocinaste	comienzan	comenzamos
cocino	cociné	comienzo	comencé

ANSWER KEY

PRESENT	PRETERITE	PRESENT	PRETERITE
Comer	**p. 42**	**Comprar**	**p. 44**
como	comimos	compro	compraste
comen	comieron	compran	compraron
come	comió	compras	compró
comemos	comieron	compramos	compré
come	comí	compra	compraron
Comprender	**p. 46**	**Conducir**	**p. 48**
comprende	comprendí	conduce	condujeron
comprendemos	comprendió	conduzco	conduje
comprenden	comprendimos	conducen	condujo
comprendes	comprendiste	conduce	condujiste
comprendo	comprendieron	conduces	condujeron
Conocer	**p. 50**	**Construir**	**p. 52**
conozco	conocimos	construyen	construyó
conoce	conoció	construimos	construyeron
conocemos	conociste	construye	construí
conocen	conocí	construyes	construyó
conoces	conocieron	construyo	construimos
Contestar	**p. 54**	**Correr**	**p. 56**
contesta	contestaron	corre	corrieron
contestamos	contestaste	corremos	corrió
contestan	contesté	corren	corriste
contestas	contestó	corro	corrieron
contesto	contestamos	corres	corrí
Cortar	**p. 58**	**Creer**	**p. 60**
corto	cortaste	creo	creyó
corta	cortaron	creen	creíste
cortas	corté	creemos	creyeron
cortamos	cortaron	crees	creí
cortan	cortamos	cree	creyó

ANSWER KEY

PRESENT	PRETERITE	PRESENT	PRETERITE
Cruzar	p. 62	Cubrir	p. 64
cruza	cruzó	cubrimos	cubrió
cruzamos	cruzaron	cubre	cubriste
cruzan	cruzó	cubres	cubrieron
cruzas	cruzamos	cubren	cubrimos
cruzan	crucé	cubro	cubrí
Dar	p. 66	Decir	p. 68
dan	dimos	digo	dijeron
damos	dio	dice	dijiste
da	di	decimos	dijo
doy	dieron	dicen	dijimos
das	diste	dices	dije
Dejar	p. 70	Descansar	p. 72
dejas	dejé	descansa	descansó
dejamos	dejaron	descansamos	descansaron
dejo	dejó	descansas	descansaste
dejan	dejaste	descansan	descansé
deja	dejó	descanso	descansó
Despertarse	p. 74	Dormir	p. 76
me despierto	se despertaron	duermo	durmió
se despierta	te despertaste	duermen	dormiste
te despiertas	se despertó	duermen	durmieron
se despierta	me desperté	duermes	dormí
se despiertan	nos despertamos	dormimos	dormimos
Durar	p. 78	Encontrar	p. 80
dura	duró	encuentran	encontré
duramos	duraron	encontramos	encontramos
dura	duraron	encuentra	encontraste
duran	duró	encuentro	encontró
duro	duré	encuentras	encontraron

ANSWER KEY

PRESENT	PRETERITE	PRESENT	PRETERITE
Enfermarse	**p. 82**	**Escribir**	**p. 84**
me enfermo	se enfermó	escribimos	escribieron
se enferma	se enfermaron	escribo	escribí
nos enfermamos	me enfermé	escriben	escribió
te enfermas	se enfermó	escribes	escribió
se enferman	te enfermaste	escribe	escribimos
Escuchar	**p. 86**	**Esperar**	**p. 88**
escucha	escucharon	espera	esperó
escucho	escuché	espero	esperaste
escuchamos	escuchó	esperas	esperé
escuchan	escuchamos	esperan	esperó
escuchas	escuchaste	esperamos	esperaron
Estudiar	**p. 90**	**Evitar**	**p. 92**
estudiamos	estudié	evitan	evitó
estudias	estudió	evitas	evitamos
estudia	estudiamos	evitamos	evitó
estudio	estudiaron	evita	evitaste
estudian	estudiaste	evito	evité
Fumar	**p. 94**	**Ganar**	**p. 96**
fuman	fumó	ganas	ganó
fumo	fumaste	ganamos	ganaron
fuma	fumé	gano	ganamos
fumas	fumó	ganan	gané
fumamos	fumaron	gana	ganaron
Gastar	**p. 98**	**Gritar**	**p. 100**
gastan	gastaste	grito	gritó
gastas	gastó	gritan	grité
gastamos	gastamos	gritas	gritamos
gasta	gastaron	gritamos	gritaron
gasto	gasté	grita	gritó

ANSWER KEY

PRESENT	PRETERITE	PRESENT	PRETERITE
Hablar	p. 102	Hacer	p. 104
hablas	habló	hacen	hizo
hablan	hablaste	hago	hicieron
hablo	hablamos	hacemos	hicimos
habla	hablaron	haces	hizo
hablamos	hablé	hace	hice
Ir	p. 106	Jugar	p. 108
vas	fuiste	jugamos	jugó
van	fueron	juego	jugaste
va	fui	juega	jugó
voy	fue	juegas	jugué
vamos	fueron	juegan	jugamos
Lavarse	p. 110	Leer	p. 112
se lavan	se lavaron	lee	leyeron
te lavas	se lavó	leemos	leí
nos lavamos	me lavé	leen	leímos
se lava	te lavaste	lees	leíste
me lavo	se lavaron	leo	leyeron
Levantarse	p. 114	Limpiar	p. 116
me levanto	se levantó	limpian	limpié
se levantan	nos levantamos	limpio	limpió
se levanta	se levantó	limpias	limpiaste
nos levantamos	me levanté	limpiamos	limpiamos
te levantas	se levantaron	limpia	limpiaron
Llamar	p. 118	Llegar	p. 120
llamo	llamaste	llegan	llegó
llamamos	llamaron	llegamos	llegaron
llaman	llamé	llego	llegaste
llamas	llamó	llegas	llegamos
llama	llamaron	llega	llegué

ANSWER KEY

PRESENT	PRETERITE	PRESENT	PRETERITE
Llevar	**p. 122**	**Mandar**	**p. 124**
llevamos	llevó	manda	mandó
lleva	llevaron	mandamos	mandaron
llevan	llevaron	manda	mandaron
llevas	llevé	mandas	mandaste
llevo	llevó	mando	mandé
Meter	**p. 126**	**Mirar**	**p. 128**
mete	metió	miran	miró
metes	metiste	miro	miramos
mete	metí	mira	miré
meto	metimos	miras	miraste
metemos	metió	miran	miraron
Nadar	**p. 130**	**Odiar**	**p. 132**
nado	nadaron	odio	odió
nadan	nadamos	odiamos	odiamos
nadamos	nadaste	odia	odiaron
nadan	nadó	odias	odiaste
nada	nadé	odia	odió
Oír	**p. 134**	**Pagar**	**p. 136**
oyen	oyó	paga	pagó
oímos	oyeron	pagamos	pagaron
oyes	oíste	paga	pagó
oigo	oyeron	pagas	pagaron
oye	oí	pago	pagué
Parar	**p. 138**	**Pedir**	**p. 140**
paran	paró	pides	pidieron
paro	paramos	pide	pidió
paramos	paré	pedimos	pedí
para	paraste	pido	pidió
paras	paró	piden	pedimos

ANSWER KEY

PRESENT	PRETERITE	PRESENT	PRETERITE
Pegar	p. 142	Pensar	p. 144
pegas	pegué	piensa	pensé
pegan	pegó	pienso	pensamos
pego	pegaron	pensamos	pensaste
pega	pegaste	piensan	pensaron
pegamos	pegamos	piensas	pensó
Perder	p. 146	Poner	p. 148
perdemos	perdiste	pone	puso
pierdo	perdí	ponemos	pusieron
pierden	perdieron	pone	puse
pierde	perdimos	pones	pusieron
pierde	perdieron	pongo	puso
Preguntar	p. 150	Prometer	p. 152
pregunta	preguntaron	prometen	prometió
pregunto	preguntó	prometo	prometió
preguntan	preguntaste	prometes	prometiste
preguntas	preguntó	promete	prometimos
preguntamos	pregunté	prometemos	prometí
Querer	p. 154	Recibir	p. 156
quiere	quisieron	recibes	recibió
queremos	quisimos	recibe	recibí
quiero	quise	recibimos	recibiste
quieren	quiso	reciben	recibimos
quieren	quisiste	recibo	recibieron
Recordar	p. 158	Robar	p. 160
recuerdo	recordaron	robamos	robó
recordamos	recordaste	robo	robaste
recuerdan	recordaron	roba	robé
recuerda	recordamos	robas	robaron
recuerdas	recordé	roban	robó

ANSWER KEY

PRESENT	PRETERITE	PRESENT	PRETERITE
Saber	**p. 162**	**Sacar**	**p. 164**
sé	supo	saco	sacó
saben	supe	sacas	sacaste
sabemos	supieron	saca	sacamos
sabes	supiste	sacamos	saqué
sabe	supimos	saca	sacaron
Salir	**p. 166**	**Saludar**	**p. 168**
salen	salió	saludo	saludaste
salimos	salí	saludan	saludó
salgo	salieron	saludas	saludamos
sales	salimos	saludan	saludó
sale	salieron	saludamos	saludé
Subir	**p. 170**	**Suspender**	**p. 172**
subimos	subieron	suspenden	suspendiste
subes	subí	suspendemos	suspendió
suben	subimos	suspendo	suspendimos
sube	subiste	suspende	suspendí
subo	subió	suspendes	suspendieron
Tener	**p. 174**	**Terminar**	**p. 176**
tengo	tuvo	termina	terminamos
tienen	tuvieron	terminan	terminé
tienes	tuvimos	termino	terminaste
tienen	tuviste	terminas	terminaron
tenemos	tuvo	terminamos	terminó
Tirar	**p. 178**	**Tocar**	**p. 180**
tira	tiré	toca	tocaste
tiramos	tiraron	toco	tocaron
tiras	tiraste	tocamos	toqué
tiran	tiró	tocas	tocamos
tira	tiramos	toca	tocó

ANSWER KEY

PRESENT	PRETERITE	PRESENT	PRETERITE
Tomar	**p. 182**	**Trabajar**	**p. 184**
tomo	tomó	trabaja	trabajó
tomamos	tomé	trabajamos	trabajaron
toman	tomaste	trabaja	trabajé
toma	tomaron	trabajas	trabajaron
tomas	tomamos	trabajo	trabajaste
Traer	**p. 186**	**Vender**	**p. 188**
traen	trajeron	vendo	vendió
traigo	trajiste	vendes	vendiste
traemos	trajimos	vendemos	vendí
traes	traje	venden	vendimos
trae	trajo	venden	vendió
Venir	**p. 190**	**Ver**	**p. 192**
viene	vinieron	ven	vio
venimos	viniste	ve	vi
vengo	vinimos	vemos	vieron
vienes	vino	veo	vio
vienen	vino	ves	vimos
Viajar	**p. 194**	**Vivir**	**p. 196**
viajan	viajó	vivo	viviste
viajo	viajaron	viven	vivimos
viajas	viajamos	vives	viví
viajamos	viajaste	viven	vivió
viajan	viajé	vive	vivieron
Volar	**p. 198**	**Volver**	**p. 200**
vuelo	volaste	vuelve	volvieron
vuelas	voló	volvemos	volviste
vuelan	volamos	vuelven	volvió
vuelan	voló	vuelve	volvimos
volamos	volé	vuelves	volví

TEACHERS' ACTIVITIES

Please visit our website at www.comicmnemonics.com for some games to play with your students. There are sheets and diagrams that can be downloaded to help you get started.

If you come up with another game that you like, please feel free to send it to us and we will post it on the website along with your name and school.

FREE COPY

Be creative—and get a full refund
on the price of this book!

Here's our challenge to you: if you can invent a better mnemonic phrase in this book—or any common Spanish verb—send it to us. If we choose it for the next edition, we'll not only credit you in print, but we'll send you a check for the full retail price!

Just follow the format: a cue word that has the beginning of the Spanish verb, a sentence that includes the definition—and can be shown by a simple drawing.

Be quick!
If more than one person sends the same idea,
the first submission wins the refund.
Send your suggestions to
submissions@alacanpublishing.com

ORDER FORM

To order copies of Comic Mnemonics using a credit card, call 1-775-827-8654,
email us at sales@beaglebay.com or fax your order to 1-775-827-8633.
Or copy and mail this order form to:

Comic Mnemonics
c/o Beagle Bay, Inc.
14120 Saddlebow Dr.
Reno, NV 89511

Your Name _____

Address _____

_____

City & State _____

Zip _____

Phone Number _____

Discount Schedule for quantity orders:

1 - 2 copies	No Discount ($16.95 ea)	
3 - 5 copies	20% ($13.56 ea)	
6 + copies	40% ($10.17 ea)	

Please send me _____ copies of Comic Mnemonics

at $_____ each for a total of $ _____

Add $4.00 shipping for the first book $ _____

Plus $1.00 for each additional book $ _____

SUBTOTAL $ _____

NV residents, please add 7.725% Sales Tax $ _____

TOTAL $ _____

_____ Check Enclosed (made payable to Beagle Bay, Inc.)

_____ Please charge my _____ Visa or _____ MasterCard

Card #_____

Expiration Date: _____ / _____   CVV2 (on back) _____

Signature: _____